Richard Cosway

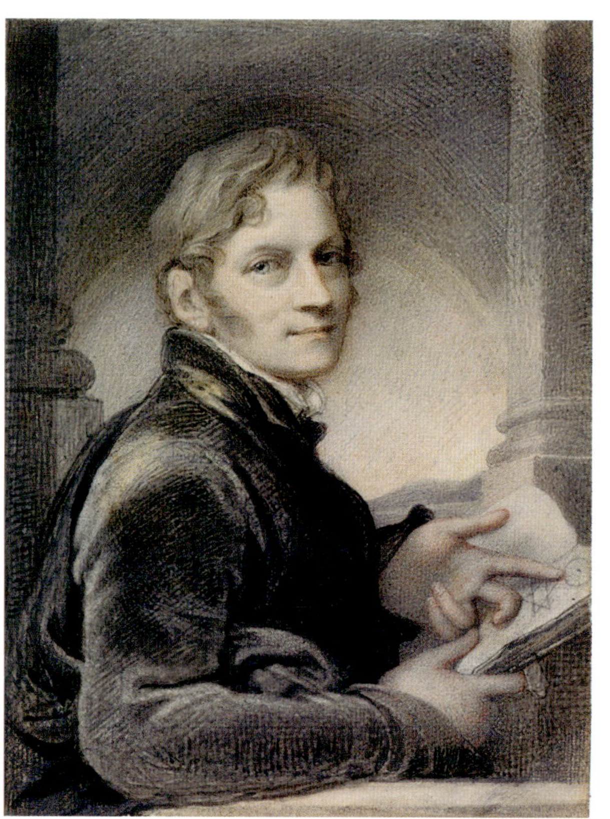

RICHARD COSWAY

Stephen Lloyd

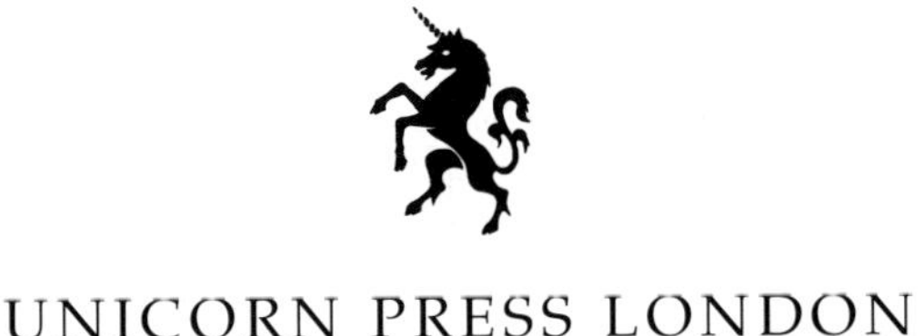

UNICORN PRESS LONDON

For Carol Colburn Høgel

Acknowledgement and thanks are due to
M.P. Ethelston for his financial assistance with this publication.

All works are by Richard Cosway and, unless stated otherwise, are oval and painted in water-colour on ivory, with the measurement being given for the height of the painted surface.

COVER *Georgiana, Duchess of Devonshire*, 1786, 8.9 cm, © The Devonshire Collection, Chatsworth. Reproduced by permission of the Chatsworth Settlement Trustees.

FRONTISPIECE *Self-portrait as a Mystic*, c.1810, pencil and watercolour on paper, 10.8 x 7.9 cm, Worcester Art Museum, Massachusetts

Unicorn Press, 76 Great Suffolk Street, London SE1 OBL
email: unicornpress@btinternet.com

First published by Unicorn Press 2005

General Editor Christopher Lloyd

ISBN 0 906290 81 3

Designed by Gillian Greenwood
Printed and bound in Slovenia for Compass Press Limited

Contents

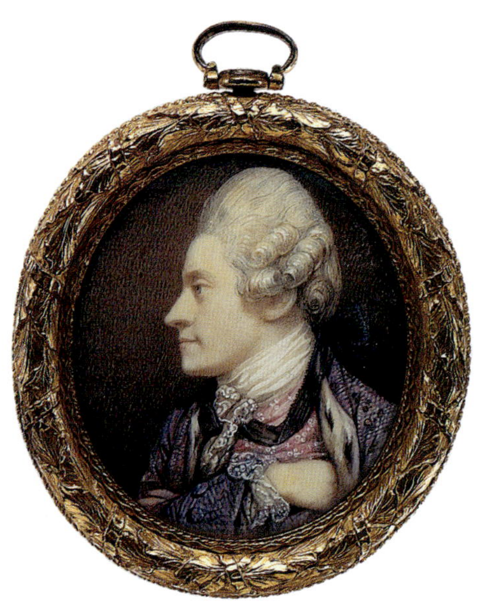

Primarius Pictor
   The miniature portraitist and virtuoso Richard Cosway
   (1742–1821)

For over three centuries from the early sixteenth century, small-scale
portraiture flourished in Britain as a result of the work of a succession of
famous miniaturists. The Tudor court of Henry VIII encouraged the
development of the art form by employing the Continental masters
Lucas Horenbout and Hans Holbein the Younger. The glittering courts of
Elizabeth I and of James VI and I were celebrated in the work of Nicholas
Hilliard and his brilliant pupil Isaac Oliver. Meanwhile the turbulent
decades of the mid-seventeenth century – marked by Charles I's
disastrous reign, Cromwell's Protectorate and Charles II's Restoration –
were illuminated by John Hoskins and his outstanding nephew and pupil,
Samuel Cooper.
   The establishment of the Hanoverian dynasty in the early eighteenth
century witnessed important technical changes to the painting of
miniatures, with the increasing popularity of enamel painting on copper,
alongside the demise of vellum as a paint surface in favour of the more
fashionable ivory. The reign of George III during the second half of the
century saw the emergence of a cluster of fine miniaturists – including
Jeremiah Meyer, John Smart, Richard Cosway and George Engleheart –
who mastered this difficult medium in their very different styles. The early

1

decades of the nineteenth century were dominated by the sober work of the Scot Andrew Robertson, while the first part of Queen Victoria's reign was marked by the confident oeuvre of Sir William Charles Ross, before the advent of photography virtually destroyed miniature painting as a profession.

Richard Cosway (1742–1821) was admired in his lifetime – and has been ever since – for the beauty and elegance with which he transformed the sitters in his portrait miniatures. These representations, which are both glamorous and intimate, can be seen as the mirror in which elite Regency society saw itself reflected. As was noted by the essayist William Hazlitt, who was the artist's most sensitive critic, these miniatures 'were not fashionable – they were fashion itself'.[1] However, Cosway's justifiable fame as a portraitist should be seen alongside his wider artistic achievement and significance as a collector and virtuoso.

Richard Cosway was baptised in the parish church of Oakford, near Tiverton in Devon, on 5 November 1742, shortly after his birth, the exact date of which is not known. His parents were named as Richard and Mary, and his father was a schoolmaster in Tiverton. It does not appear that Cosway had any other brothers or sisters. As a child Cosway must have shown signs of talent as a draughtsman, and when he was a young teenager it was decided that he should further his artistic studies in London. In this venture he may well have been supported by his uncle, who had been a mayor of Tiverton, and by Oliver Peard, a leading merchant in this significant wool town.

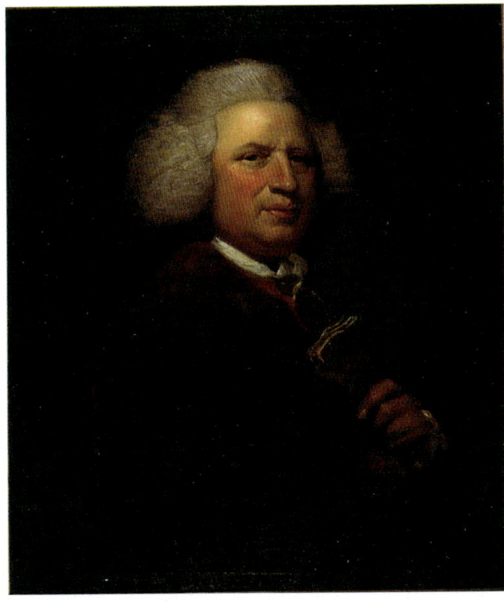

FIG.1 Richard Cosway,
William Shipley, 1759–60,
oil on canvas, RSA, London.

Cosway was sent up to London at the end of 1754 to study under
William Shipley (FIG.1), a drawing master and portraitist, who had
recently established himself in the capital. He had just launched the
Society for the Encouragement of Arts, Manufactures and Commerce
(soon to be known informally as the Society of Arts) and was attracting
talented young students. In the inaugural competition held by the

Society in 1755 Cosway won the first prize of £5 in the category of under-fourteen-year-olds for drawing the subject 'Compassion' after an original by Charles Le Brun; he was to win other awards for drawing in the following few years. Fellow students from this period who also went on to enjoy successful careers included the portrait miniaturists John Smart, Ozias Humphry and Richard Crosse, the painters William Hodges, Francis Wheatley and John Hamilton Mortimer, and the sculptor Joseph Nollekens. This group of artists were trained in various aspects of draughtsmanship, in particular copying from prints and the casts of famous classical sculptures. Cosway had also begun to train as a portraitist – in oils and miniatures – under the auspices of Shipley, to whom he became apprenticed and with whom he lived off the Strand. One of his finest early miniatures, *Thomas Cosway* (MINIATURE 1A) – painted in the neat style of the so-called 'modest school' – was of his uncle or cousin, and is datable to around 1760. In the same year Cosway exhibited a confident head-and-shoulders oil portrait of his mentor William Shipley at the inaugural public exhibition of the Society of Artists.[2] (FIG.1) This significant pictorial statement, influenced by the oil paintings of Thomas Hudson and Sir Joshua Reynolds, marked Cosway's emergence as a young artist.

Throughout the 1760s Cosway exhibited his work – oils, miniatures and drawings – publicly in London, both at the Free Society of Artists from 1761 to 1764 and again two years later, while from 1767 to 1769 he returned to showing at the Society of Artists. Very few of his works from

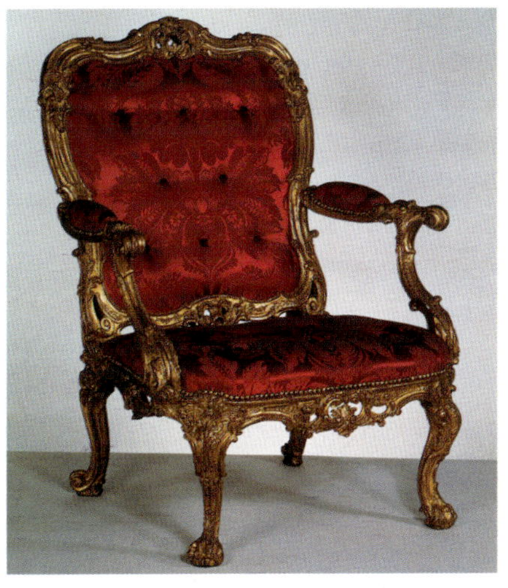

this decade have survived. An exception is the ambitious and large portrait miniature of an actress, *Miss Elliot in the character of Pallas or Minerva* (MINIATURE 3), which was shown at the Society of Artists in 1769. Two years earlier Cosway's unlocated miniature of Mrs Draper had been praised by her literary admirer, Laurence Sterne, in his famous work *The Journal to Eliza*. In 1775 the artist portrayed the same sitter in an oil painting; here she is shown seated in his spectacular sitters' chair, which was designed by Matthias Lock and is datable to *c*.1755–60 (FIG.2). This bold piece of studio furniture indicated Cosway's increasing confidence

5

and flamboyant artistic persona. Well known as a high-profile 'macaroni' or dandy at this period, he painted himself wearing fashionable 'Vandyke' dress both in MINATURE 4 and in an oil painting.[3] Cosway's status as a society artist was consolidated by his move to the heart of the fashionable West End. From 1768 he rented the studio and house of the recently deceased oil portraitist John Shackleton (Principal Painter to George II) at 4 Berkeley Street or Row, just off Piccadilly, where he lived and worked until 1784.

In 1769 Cosway was admitted as a student to the schools of the newly founded Royal Academy of Arts. The following year he exhibited three oil paintings there, and he was elected an associate academician. In 1771 he displayed a further three oils and a miniature, and he was elected Royal Academician. Cosway continued to show his ambitious oil portraiture at the Academy's annual exhibitions (1770–87, 1798–1800, 1803 and 1806), rather than his more fashionable and prolific output of portrait miniatures and drawings.

A number of Cosway's little-studied oil paintings from the 1770s survive. These include *The Witts Family*, an unusual conversation piece that serves both as an allegory and as a memorial. It was exhibited at the Royal Academy in 1770 as *The portraits of a gentleman, his wife, and sister, in the character of Fortitude introducing Hope as the companion to Distress.* Equally influenced by the work of Sir Joshua Reynolds was Cosway's allegorical oil *The Carrick Family*.[4] Displayed at the Academy the following year as *A lady and her daughters in the character of Virtue and Beauty directed by Wisdom to sacrifice at the altar of Diana*, it was engraved in mezzotint by J. R. Smith in 1773.

Perhaps Cosway's most successful painting from this decade was one that was not exhibited publicly. This was a conversation piece painted in 1771–5, *Charles Townley with a Group of Connoisseurs*. Letters from the artist to Charles Townley (1737–1805), the important collector of classical sculptures, reveal their close friendship and the lascivious interests of this circle of connoisseurs, who are shown in the picture admiring two statues of the nude Venus. Cosway resisted Townley's invitations to join him in Italy – probably owing to pressure of work – but the artist's sympathy for Italy was revealed in a letter to Townley – then in Italy – dated 24 February 1772: 'Italy for ever say I – if the Italian women fuck as well in Italy as they do here, you must be happy indeed – I am such a zealot for them, that I'll be damned if I ever fuck an English woman again (if I can help it)'. Curiously, unlike so many of his artistic contemporaries, the artist never visited Italy. This letter, with its emphatic statement of Cosway's sexuality, explicitly contradicts later historians' suggestions that the artist was homosexual. As to Cosway's character, the critic William Hazlitt – in his brilliant descriptive cameo of the artist – recorded that his future wife Maria, when questioned in Paris during 1802 about her husband, stated that he was 'toujours riant, toujours gai'.[5]

In 1780 two events occurred that were to transform Cosway's already successful career as a fashionable society artist in London. This was the year that he met his future wife, Maria Hadfield (1760–1838), a talented

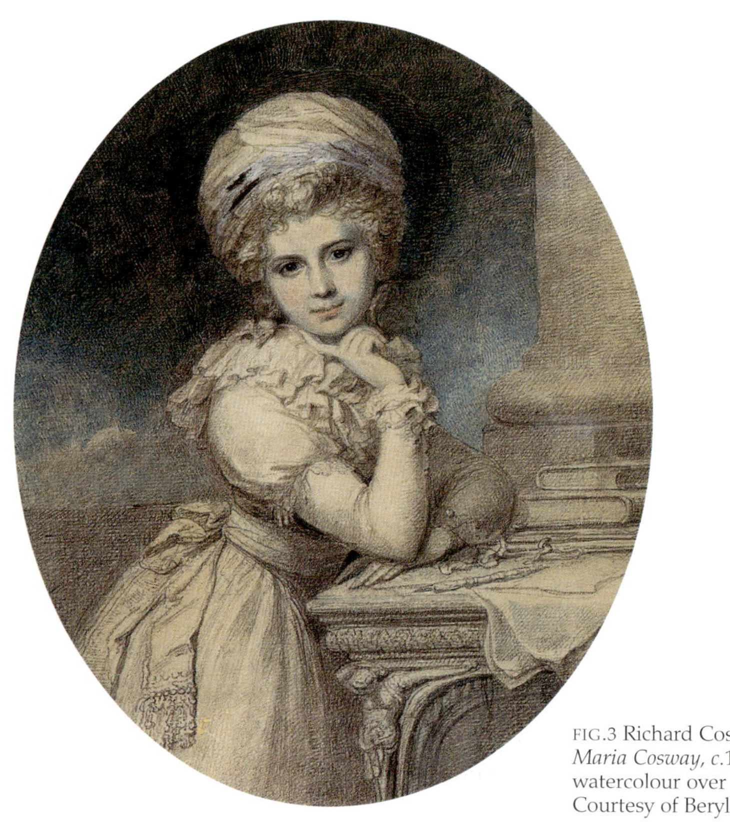

FIG.3 Richard Cosway,
*Maria Cosway, c.*1780–5,
watercolour over pencil.
Courtesy of Beryl Kendall.

artist and musician who had recently arrived in the metropolis from her native Florence (FIG.3). It was also the year that he first portrayed in miniature George, Prince of Wales (1762–1830), later George IV, who had just turned eighteen and who was to become Cosway's most important patron over the next three decades.

Cosway's marriage appears to have been brokered by Charles Townley, who knew the Hadfield family in Florence, and who protected them in London, and also by Maria's mother Isabella, who was looking to arrange a financially secure future for her daughter. In later life Maria recalled the situation in her autobiographical letter of 24 May 1830 to Richard's cousin, Sir William Cosway: 'I became acquainted with Mr. Cosway, his offer was Accepted, my mother's wishes gratified, and I married tho' under Age'.[6] It is very likely that Richard settled the considerable sum of £2800 on his new wife. The couple were married at the prominent church of St George's, Hanover Square, London, on 18 January 1781. Her father having died in 1776, Maria was given away in marriage by Charles Townley.

Throughout the 1780s the Cosways established an intensely fashionable salon, firstly in Berkeley Street, and then after 1784 at their new home in the central apartment of Schomberg House in Pall Mall, where Thomas Gainsborough and his family were their immediate neighbours in the west wing (FIG.4). Maria was the centre of attention as a beautiful and charismatic hostess, and as a musician who sang and performed on the harp as well as on other keyboard instruments at her much sought-after concerts. The *bon ton* of international and aristocratic society was attracted to these events. Richard was thus able to increase his portraiture business – especially for portrait miniatures – at the elite end of the market. By adorning his residences with his varied and extensive collections, he was also able to advertise his status and ability as a notable connoisseur and collector of old master paintings and decorative arts.

Twenty years older than the Prince of Wales when he first sat to the artist, Cosway not only helped create a fashionable and intimate pictorial image for the increasingly dissolute heir to the throne, but he also assisted in forming his young patron's aesthetic taste. The extensive manuscript list of unpaid portraits drawn up towards the end of Cosway's life in 1820 (debts that were in fact settled later that year) showed that the prince regularly commissioned work from the artist during the period 1780 to 1808.[7] These were chiefly portraits of the prince, mainly miniatures – sometimes of eyes – but also drawings and paintings. There were also commissioned portraits of the prince's lovers – in particular of Mary, Mrs 'Perdita' Robinson and of Maria, Mrs Fitzherbert – as well as of most members of his family and close friends. In 1785 the prince allowed Cosway to sign his work with the extravagant Latin title *Primarius Pictor Serenissimi Walliae Principis* ('Principal Painter to his Royal Highness the Prince of Wales'). Thereafter the miniatures were mostly signed this way on the back, with the finished portrait drawings being inscribed on the front and underneath the image. The Royal Collection holds the finest and most extensive collection of Cosway's miniatures of the Prince of Wales and his family. Other particularly important groups of the artist's

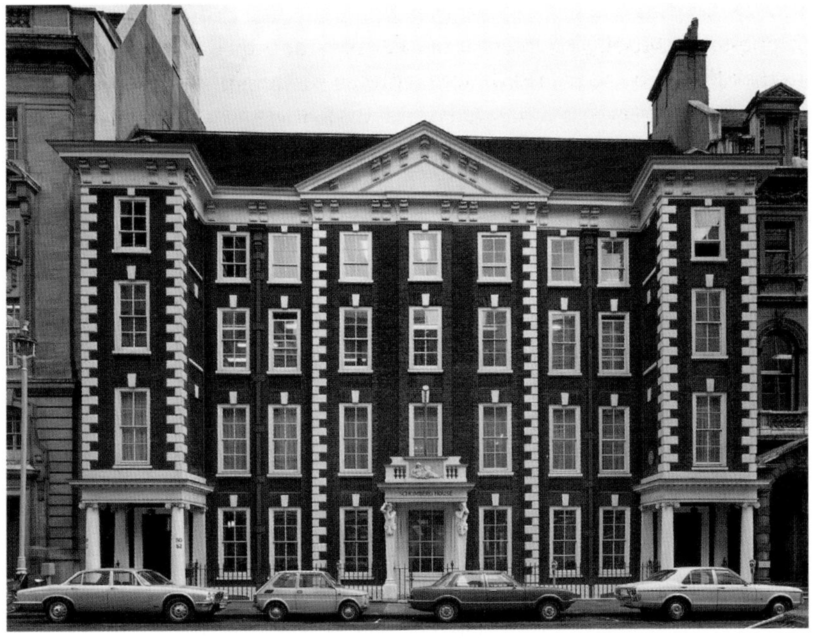

FIG.4 Schomberg House, 80–82 Pall Mall, London, façade built 1698,
photograph courtesy of GE Capital Corporation Estates Ltd

small-scale work can be found in the Victoria and Albert Museum in
London, the Fitzwilliam Museum in Cambridge, and at the Huntington
Library and Art Collections in San Marino, California.

11

Cosway's mature style of miniature painting, which had emerged by 1785, can be described as the epitome of early Regency taste. Following on from the technical developments made by Jeremiah Meyer in the 1770s, Cosway expanded the size of the miniature portrait to around three inches in height. Like Meyer, he fully exploited the inherent luminosity of the ivory support allied to the natural translucency of watercolour. Cosway also developed highly characteristic compositional and technical traits that made his portrait miniatures notably alluring and flattering, often for a young and wealthy adult clientele. He enlarged the eyes within the head, and increased the size of the head in comparison with the body. He incorporated brilliant sky-blue and white cloudy back-grounds, thus enhancing the viewer's focus on the head and eyes of the sitter. He also pioneered a bravura technique that contrasted delicate stipple work in the face with more linear and expressive brushwork for the body and the sky. Two of the finest examples of his work from this period are an *Unknown Lady*, formerly entitled *Mrs Fitzherbert* (MINIATURE 16), datable to *c*.1785–90 and *Madame du Barry*, dated 1791.[8]

The most vivid contemporary account of sitting to Cosway for a portrait miniature is provided by the diarist William Hickey. He recorded the apparently effortless portrayal by the artist of his mistress Charlotte Barry in December 1781: 'Then presenting his hand he led her into his painting room, rubbed out the elegantly arranged hair, and drew her exactly as she then sat before me, making as he had truly predicted one of the most beautiful pictures I ever beheld, the likeness being inimitable. After sitting full three hours, I saw evidently that he was greatly delighted with it himself. With some difficulty I prevailed upon him not to touch it any more, feeling satisfied it could not be improved and might be hurt by attempting at a higher finishing. I would willingly have carried it away at that time, but that he would not hear of, saying he must touch the drapery a little, besides which he was too proud of his performance not to be desirous of showing it to a few persons who were real connoisseurs. A week afterwards I received it from Cosway, and it has ever since been my inseparable companion'.[9]

Cosway enjoyed great facility as a painter and draughtsman, and was a notably prolific artist, allegedly being able to undertake up to twelve separate portrait sittings a day for miniatures. During the 1790s and early 1800s, as he matured as an artist, his work lost some of its earlier brilliance but became more subtle, both in characterisation and in execution. He was particularly adept at the combined use of monochrome shading and increasingly limited application of pigment, especially in the sky backgrounds, which lends these portraits considerable psychological complexity. Outstanding examples of Cosway's late miniatures are *Arthur Wellesley, later 1st Duke of Wellington* (MINIATURE 28), signed and dated 1808; the actor *John Philip Kemble* (MINIATURE 29); and the artist's last *Self-portrait* (MINIATURE 30), both of which are datable to *c*.1810.

Cosway's mature style of miniature painting of the 1780s and 1790s had a profound influence on a number of his contemporaries. He trained the two brothers Nathaniel Plimer (1757–1822) and Andrew Plimer

(1763–1837), who both seem to have worked for Cosway in the early 1780s. Among the more successful artists who adopted aspects of Cosway's style were Charlotte Jones (1768–1847), William Wood (1769–1810) and Mrs Joseph Mee, née Anne Foldsone, (*c*.1770/5–1851).

Alongside his lucrative business as a portrait miniaturist, Cosway developed in parallel his production of small-scale full-length portrait drawings, which were known as 'stained' or 'tinted' drawings, and which were to be highly influential on other artists such as Henry Edridge, Adam Buck and George Chinnery. These drawings on paper were priced by Cosway at the same level as his miniatures, namely thirty guineas from the 1780s. In such portraits the head was executed in detailed watercolour, while more fluid draughtsmanship in graphite was used for the body and the background landscape. Cosway produced these portrait drawings in considerable numbers between about 1790 and 1810. Particularly fine examples from the 1790s are *Princess Natalia Petrovna Galitzine with her two daughters Ekaterina and Sophia*, dated 1795, and *Caroline, Princess of Wales with her daughter Princess Charlotte*, dated 1797, both of which were commissioned by the Prince of Wales.[10]

Cosway's self-portraits on paper are remarkable statements of his technical virtuosity as a draughtsman. The *Self-portrait with Busts of Michelangelo and Rubens*, datable to *c*.1789 – a richly detailed full-length composition in pen and ink – is a complex artistic manifesto, in which Cosway presents himself as a sophisticated Rubensian courtier-artist and virtuoso. As a pendant to this is his equally rich study *Maria Cosway with*

14

a Bust of Leonardo da Vinci. About 1800 Richard drew himself in a searching *Self-portrait Leaning on his Hand*, which is reminiscent of work by Henry Fuseli.[11]

Cosway was a prolific draughtsman throughout his career, and works on paper by him can be found in many British, European and American museums. One complete sketchbook with 119 drawings is preserved in the British Museum, London. Around 700 separate sheets are held in the Fondazione Cosway at Lodi near Milan, where they had been taken by Maria Cosway in 1822, the year after her husband's death. These drawings can be grouped into various categories, whether finished works or compositional sketches: studies for portraits; figure studies; classical, allegorical and historical scenes; religious imagery; angels, motherhood and children. Cosway worked in various media, usually pen and ink or graphite, though occasionally in black chalk or sometimes adding wash or watercolour.

Two key early subject drawings by Cosway are the rococo fantasy in watercolours of *Rinaldo and Armida* (*c*.1772) and the dramatic Fuselian *Perseus and Medusa*, which is more monochromatic and can be dated to the second half of the 1780s. The former work is directly related to a small oil panel exhibited at the Royal Academy that year. Both drawings were acquired by Duke Albert von Sachsen-Teschen sometime after 1785 but during Cosway's lifetime. The artist's major achievement as a draughtsman during the 1790s was the series of at least ten pen-and-ink drawings illustrating Musaeus's classical poem *Hero and Leander*, using

Sir Robert Stapylton's translation of 1647, Cosway's copy of which survives. Especially notable for their intense fusion of classical, Renaissance and neoclassical motifs are *Hero and Leander in the Temple, Hero and Leander by the Hellespont* and *Hero's Dream*. After 1800 Cosway increasingly turned to graphite interpretations of religious subjects from the New Testament, striving to fuse a profound spirituality with a close study of the work of Correggio and the late drawings of Michelangelo. The over-heated merging of these stylistic concerns is clearly seen in the late, masterly drawing *The Death of Leonardo da Vinci in the Arms of Francis I*, datable to *c*.1815.[12]

It appears that Cosway also drew for his own pleasure. The portfolios of his own drawings were intended to be seen – by himself and his close artist and collector friends – alongside his famous collection of Old Master drawings. Certainly this was how the two collections of drawings were appreciated by Sir Thomas Lawrence. After seeing these works in 1811, Lawrence wrote revealingly to his friend, the artist Joseph Farington, reappraising Cosway: 'What are Mr Phillips, and Mr Owen, and Sir William Beechey, and Mr Shee's in mere colouring, when compar'd to the knowledge – the familiar acquaintance with, study; and often happy appropriation and even liberal imitation of the Old Masters, the fix'd Landmark of Art, of this little Being [Cosway] which we have been accustom'd never to think or speak of but with contempt?'[13]

Like most of his contemporary artists, Cosway collaborated with reproductive engravers to promote his subject compositions and portraits, whether miniatures, drawings or oil paintings. Throughout the artist's more than fifty-year-long career 163 separate prints were produced from his compositions. Cosway tended to have some of his oil paintings reproduced in the heavy tonal contrast of mezzotint, as with the baroque pastiche *Europa*, engraved by J.R.Smith in 1776, or the dramatic *Lady Hume*, engraved by V.Green in 1783. The artist's more delicate miniatures and drawings were engraved in the fashionable stipple manner by, among others, F.Bartolozzi, L.Schiavonetti, the Condé brothers, A.Cardon and J.Agar. Occasionally Cosway worked with the line engravers, notably William Sharp, who reproduced four of Cosway's compositions, including three miniatures: *George, Prince of Wales* (1790), his brother *William, Duke of Clarence* (1791) and the Scottish lawyer, later Lord Chancellor, *The Hon. Thomas Erskine* (also 1791). Sharp also engraved Cosway's unlocated religious composition of *Christ's Passion*, which was commissioned in 1791 for Thomas Macklin's great project of an engraved Bible.

Some of Cosway's more sentimental subjects were reproduced during the 1780s by commercial stipple engravers such as Francesco Bartolozzi, as well as by Jean Condé (d.1794) – a pupil of Jacques-Louis David – and his younger brother Pierre Condé (1767/8–1840). The key instance of this type of composition and reproduction was Cosway's mannered and erotic *Docet Amor* or *The Origin of Painting*, which was engraved by J.Condé and pub-lished by Cosway himself in 1791. The latter was an image of iconographical significance for Cosway as he used it as the frontispiece for the private contract sale catalogue of his Old Master paintings also published that year.

Three series of drawings by Cosway were engraved and published, two during his lifetime and one posthumously. In 1785 six of the artist's compositions on educational subjects were engraved in the chalk manner. In 1800 about forty of his subject drawings were reproduced as soft-ground etchings by his wife Maria, and were published by Rudolph Ackermann as a drawing book, titled *Imitations in Chalk*. In order to promote her late husband's artistic reputation in Italy, Maria engaged the line engraver Giovanni Paolo Lasinio to reproduce fifteen of Richard's drawings, which she then had published in Florence during 1826 as *Disegni scelti dai portafogli del celebre Riccardo Cosway*.

Cosway was an outstanding and highly respected collector, connoisseur and virtuoso of the late eighteenth and early nineteenth centuries, though his two collections of Old Master paintings were not as important as that of Reynolds, nor his extensive assemblage of Old Master prints and over 2500 drawings as remarkable as that of Lawrence. Nevertheless, Cosway was a wealthy artist-collector, who sought out paintings and works on paper of the finest quality and interest by the main artists of the Italian Renaissance and the Flemish and Dutch seventeenth-century schools.

Among Cosway's most important paintings, prints and drawings were a number by his greatest artistic hero, Rubens. These included the oil sketches *King James VI and I uniting the Kingdoms of Scotland* and *The Rape of Ganymede*. Cosway also owned the large canvas *A View of the Escorial*, then thought to be by Rubens, but now considered to have been painted

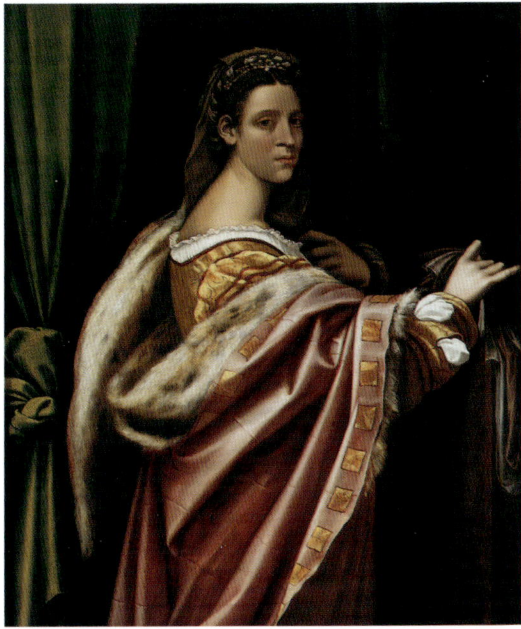

by Pieter Verhulst from a sketch by Rubens. In 1791 Cosway sold it to his patron Lord Radnor. Similarly, the artist sold Lord Radnor a major high Renaissance portrait on panel, then thought to be by Raphael of his mistress 'La Fornarina', although since universally reattributed to Sebastiano del Piombo (FIG.5).[14]

19

Cosway also collected the work of Rembrandt. He owned Rembrandt's painting *A Franciscan Friar* and the highly important *Mountainous Landscape* by Hercules Seghers, which Rembrandt had once owned and retouched. Among the Rembrandt drawings in Cosway's possession the most significant were the *Study after Leonardo's 'Last Supper'* and the portrait sketch of Jan Six. Probably the most curious panel painting in Cosway's collection was *The Mass of St Giles* by an anonymous Franco-Flemish master, working around 1500. Cosway considered this work, which was highly unusual for the taste of the period, to be by Jan Gossaert (called Mabuse) and to represent 'St Thomas Aquinas performing mass in the abbey of St Denis'.[15] Apart from his 1791 private contract sale and catalogue of almost five hundred paintings, the rest of his picture collection was sold at auction in London by Christie's on 2–3 March 1792. The collection that Cosway subsequently formed was auctioned by George Stanley in two main sales on 17–19 May 1821 and on 8–9 March 1822, just before and just after the artist's death.

Cosway also had an extraordinary eye for furniture, decorative arts, sculpture and armour, in particular items that were highly decorated and were said to have historical associations. Sir John Soane, who was a close friend of both the Cosways, bought a number of objets d'art and sculptures from the posthumous sale of Richard's collection, *A Catalogue of the very curious and valuable Assemblage of Miscellaneous Articles of Taste and Virtù*, held at George Stanley's on 22–24 May 1821. Soane purchased terracotta statuettes of Charles II by Arnold Quellin and of James Craggs the younger by Giovanni Battista Guelfi in addition to small classical bronzes. Some of these purchases can be identified among the objects still to be found in the Sir John Soane Museum, London. Cosway also owned a very precious piece of Elizabethan silver-gilt, now known as the Cosway Salt. The art critic J. T. Smith described the effects of the interiors at Stratford Place, off Oxford Street, where Cosway had moved in 1791: 'His new house he fitted up in so picturesque, and, indeed, so princely a style, that I regret drawings were not made of the general appearance of each apartment; for many of the rooms were more like scenes of enchantment, pencilled by a poet's fancy than anything, perhaps, before displayed in a domestic habitation'.[16]

In 1822 William Hazlitt equally praised the taste and artistic imagination of 'Fancy's Child' – as he referred to Cosway – in his well-known appreciation (at the expense of William Beckford's 'desert of magnificence' at Fonthill Abbey) of the collections and interiors at Stratford Place: 'What a fairy palace was his of specimens of art, antiquarianism and *virtù* jumbled all together in the richest disorder, dusty, shadowy, obscure with much left to the imagination (how different from the finical, polished, petty, perfect, modernized air of *Fonthill!*).'[17]

Arguably Cosway's greatest success as a collector and connoisseur was achieved during the couple's socially triumphant visit to Paris in the summer of 1786. (They returned to London in October that year after a further art-buying tour of Flemish towns and cities.) This visit is now remembered for Maria's affair with Thomas Jefferson, who was then based in Paris as the American Minister to France. Cosway was ostensibly working on a commission from the Prince of Wales's great friend, Louis-Philippe, duc d'Orléans (later known as Philippe-Egalité) to portray his children in a drawing. Through his friendship with the antiquarian and adventurer, baron d'Hancarville, however, Cosway conceived the idea of presenting to Louis XVI – for display in the Grande Galerie of the Louvre – the four huge tapestry cartoons that he owned. At the time these were thought to be by Raphael and Giulio Romano and to be part of the *History of Camillus* tapestry series. (They are now thought to have been made by Giulio Romano's studio and followers and are known to be from the *Fructus Belli* and the *History of Scipio* tapestry series.) Cosway's offer was gratefully accepted on behalf of the king by baron d'Angiviller, the Master of the King's Works. These Renaissance cartoons were widely admired by the leading French artists of the day – especially Jacques-Louis David – when they were unveiled in the Louvre in 1788.[18]

In return for Cosway's magnanimous gesture (the cartoons were thought to be worth around £10,000), on 18 July 1788 the artist was presented by Louis XVI with four superb Gobelins tapestries from the *Don Quixote* series after Charles-Antoine Coypel's designs, as well as a Savonnerie carpet. This was an exceptional gift, of a kind normally reserved by the French for visiting foreign royalty and ambassadors, and is indicative of Cosway's extraordinarily high status at this time. In 1789, Cosway in his turn made the equally splendid gift of these tapestries to his foremost patron, the Prince of Wales. They were intended for the decoration of one of the principal bedrooms at the prince's sumptuous London residence of Carlton House, and remain in the Royal Collection to this day.

On 4 May 1790 Maria Cosway gave birth to her only child, Louisa Paolina Angelica Cosway. She was partially named after her godfather the Corsican patriot General Pasquale Paoli (1725–1807), who was an intimate friend of Maria's, and who was portrayed by Cosway in a masterly Titianesque oil of 1798. Louisa was also named after her godmother Princess Louisa of Stolberg, Duchess of Albany (1753–1824), the former wife of Prince Charles Edward Stuart (1720–88). After suffering much during her pregnancy and labour, a few weeks after the birth of her daughter Maria travelled to Italy for her health, leaving Louisa in the hands of her husband, as well as her mother and her sister, Charlotte. Maria did not return to London to see her daughter or husband for another four and a half years. The full reasons for this extraordinary absence from the upbringing of Louisa – let alone Richard – are not yet known. However, Maria may have suffered some form of breakdown, since she chose to enter a convent in Genoa. Cosway made a number of portraits of Louisa, including drawn studies, but most memorably an exquisite miniature of her aged about two (MINIATURE 23).[19]

In 1791 the artist decided to move from Schomberg House. In May of that year he offered his Old Master paintings for sale by private contract. He published *A Catalogue of the Entire Collection of Pictures of Richard Cosway Esq., R.A.*, with the descriptions of the works probably written by himself. He then leased a magnificent Adam-style mansion designed in 1773–5 by Richard Edwin at 22 Stratford Place, on Oxford Street. This he filled with the residue of his art collections, to which he continued to add. Three years later, possibly owing to the lack of privacy on Oxford Street, he decided to move two doors along to 20 Stratford Place, a much quieter residence. He lived there until the last year of his life, when he rented a cottage at 31 Edgware Road.

Maria Cosway returned from Italy to her family in London in November 1794. After developing a sore throat, Louisa died of fever on 29 July 1796. Both Richard and Maria were devastated by this loss and profoundly affected. Maria confined herself to her room for weeks, and later sought solace in her Catholic faith, while developing her initial plans for the education of young girls. Cosway drew Louisa on her deathbed in a moving graphite study.[20] Her body was embalmed in a sarcophagus that was kept in the Cosway residence for some time afterwards, before its burial in Bunhill Fields to the north of the City of London.

Richard's eccentric spiritual explorations intensified after Louisa's death. He had shown considerable enthusiasm for Swedenborgianism and Mesmerism in the 1780s and 1790s, while later he became a committed faith healer and astrologer. The artist's extensive library, which was sold at auction just before his death, not only contained books on history, poetry and fine arts, but also 'a numerous Collection of early Works on Divinity' and an 'unusual assemblage of Treatises on Magic,

Necromancy, Apparitions, Vampires'. The importance of these subjects to Cosway can be seen in his two late self-portraits: the *Self-portrait as a Mystic* (frontispiece), datable to *c*.1810, and the full-length *Self-portrait as Esau*, dated 1812.[21] Both works contain overt references to the artist's deep involvement in freemasonry and religious mysticism throughout the later part of his life.

During the period *c*.1780–1815 Cosway worked for three major aristocratic patrons apart from the Prince of Wales. The first was Jacob, 2nd Earl of Radnor (1750–1826), all of whose commissions from the artist between 1781 and 1812 are recorded in his estate account book. Cosway portrayed his patron in miniature and in a full-length oil painting. He also portrayed his wife in a drawing and his children in a series of oils, the most successful of which is the charming, pastoral composition *William, 3rd Earl of Radnor, with his sister the Hon. Mary Anne Pleydell-Bouverie*.[22] The artist also sold Lord Radnor a select group of important Old Master paintings from his private contract sale of 1791, thus enhancing one of the most important aristocratic collections of paintings to be formed in Britain during the eighteenth and early nineteenth centuries.

The second key aristocratic client of Cosway's was William, 3rd Viscount Courtenay (1768–1835), the young lover ('Kitty') of William Beckford. The portraits commissioned from the artist by Lord Courtenay between 1790 and 1812 – as noted in the artist's list of outstanding bills – were not paid for until 1820. This list refers to many miniatures as well as an important group of full-length oils. Most notable are the extravagant, 'Vandyke' fancy-dress portrait of Lord Courtenay, dated 1791, and the romantic, seated group of three of his sisters, *The Hons. Sophia, Louisa and Mathilda Courtenay*, dated 1806. Cosway was also commissioned to paint a large altarpiece of *The Supper at Emmaus*, in which he depicted himself in the guise of the innkeeper.[23]

The third major patron of Cosway's was George, Marquess of Blandford, later 5th Duke of Marlborough (1766–1840), a profligate bibliophile who assembled a celebrated library at his house, White-Knights, near Reading. Apart from commissioning miniatures, drawings and prints of himself and his family from 1797 to *c.*1815, Lord Blandford also sat to Cosway in 1797 for an elegant oil portrait, reminiscent of the work of Sir Peter Lely in the previous century. In addition, he ordered a spectacular double portrait of two of his children playing with armour, *George, Earl of Sunderland and his brother Lord Charles Spencer*.[24]

In 1801 Maria Cosway left her husband again to travel to Paris to copy – with his encouragement – the outstanding Old Master paintings that had recently been looted from Italy, and that were now displayed in the Grande Galerie of the Musée Central des Arts at the Louvre. In 1803, after two years in Paris, she settled in Lyons, where she established a school for girls. In 1809 that school closed, and she established a new educational establishment in Lodi, near Milan, which opened in 1812. On hearing that her husband had been taken ill in 1815, she visited London to be with him. Though they never divorced, this long separation must have been caused by the effective breakdown of their marriage. Maria returned to London in 1817 after Richard Cosway's health had weakened through a series of strokes. When he died of a seizure – in his carriage on 4 July 1821 – Maria organised a grand funeral on 12 July at St Marylebone Church, and commissioned a marble memorial including a portrait roundel from Richard Westmacott.[25]

Maria stayed another year in London, organising a series of sales of Cosway's art collections and possessions through the auctioneer George Stanley. She also attempted – unsuccessfully – to sell her husband's own drawings to George IV, and then mounted an exhibition of them at Stanley's auction room in London during the spring of 1822. After touring Scotland, she returned to Italy to resume directing her girls' school at Lodi. Having endowed it with at least £4000 from Richard's estate, the school was re-established in 1830 as the Collegio delle Dame Inglesi. Created a Baroness of the Austrian Empire in 1834, Maria Cosway died in 1838 and is buried at Lodi in the church of Santa Maria delle Grazie. In 1822 she had taken to Lodi all of her husband's surviving drawings, as well as prints, miniatures, paintings, both by him and a few of the Old Masters, and also some of his books and documents. Together with her own collection, these materials form the basis of the Fondazione Cosway at Lodi, which today cares for them after her school finally closed in 1978.

Following Cosway's death and the various sales of his collections, there was a notable lack of market interest in his work during the mid-nineteenth century. This was no doubt part of the reaction during the

27

reign of William IV and the early decades of Queen Victoria's rule to the perceived excesses of the Regency period and taste. Collectors' interest in Cosway only began to revive towards the end of the nineteenth century, when the *fin-de-siècle* mood became more attuned to the lightness of the Regency style and aesthetic – as epitomised by Cosway's miniatures. This was probably linked to the South Kensington Museum's active promotion of the portrait miniature after its great exhibition on this art form in 1865, undertaken in compensation for the demise of miniature-painting in the mid-century on account of the advent of photography. The 1890s and the first decade of the twentieth century witnessed the apogee of interest from collectors and the art market in Cosway's work. In 1890 the print dealer Frederick B. Daniell published a catalogue raisonné of prints after Richard Cosway's work. Meanwhile in 1895 there was a significant exhibition of the Cosways' work at Moncorvo House in South Kensington, which was organised by Dr George C. Williamson, a prolific writer on eighteenth-century portrait miniaturists. 1897 saw the publication of Williamson's monograph on the Cosways, with a second edition following in 1905. High prices continued to be paid for Cosway miniatures, in particular, up until the outbreak of World War II, most spectacularly at the auction in 1935 of J. Pierpont Morgan's famous collection of miniatures.[26]

In the austere years after 1945 there was a reaction against Cosway's work, which was once more seen to epitomise profligate Regency taste. As the art market for miniatures recovered in the 1960s, the naturalistic miniatures of John Smart became increasingly admired, but it was not until the 1990s that Cosway's life and work were fully reassessed with a series of publications. Notable among these was the catalogue of the 1995 exhibition *Richard and Maria Cosway* that was held at the Scottish National Portrait Gallery in Edinburgh and then travelled to the National Portrait Gallery in London. Over a hundred of Cosway's drawings, preserved at the Fondazione Cosway in Lodi, were published in 1998 in a collection of essays in Italian devoted to the Cosways.

Richard Cosway can now be seen as one of the most significant multifaceted artistic personalities active in Regency Britain. Arguably, he was the pre-eminent pupil of William Shipley, being a frequent prize-winner at the latter's newly founded Society of Arts. Cosway was also a versatile oil portraitist and a sophisticated draughtsman of subject compositions. He was undoubtedly the most important, influential, and fashionable portrait miniaturist and draughtsman active during the last two decades of the eighteenth century and the beginning of the nine-teenth; his delicate style and flattering portrayals have come to epitomise Regency society. Cosway's flamboyant personality, eccentric mysticism, and brilliant marriage to Maria Hadfield during the 1780s brought him celebrity and notoriety. He can justly be called the principal recorder of the Prince of Wales's image from 1780 to 1808, as well as having exerted significant influence on his patron's artistic taste and collecting during that period. Perhaps Cosway's greatest achievement, however, was as a connoisseur, virtuoso, and collector – particularly of Old Master paintings, prints, and drawings – who was admired and respected by some of his

most discerning contemporaries, notably the painter Sir Thomas
Lawrence, the architect Sir John Soane, the critic William Hazlitt, as well
as the collectors Francis Douce and William Beckford.

FOOTNOTES

1 Hazlitt 1822 and 1826.

2 Since 1847 the Royal Society of Arts.

3 The oil version of *Mrs Draper* is in a private collection; Cosway's sitters' chair is in
the Victoria and Albert Museum, London; and the self-portrait in oils is at
Attingham Park, Shrewsbury (National Trust).

4 *The Witts Family* is in the Tate collection, London, and *The Carrick Family* is at Castle
Coole, Enniskillen (National Trust).

5 *Charles Townley with a Group of Connoisseurs* is at Towneley Hall Art Gallery and
Museums, Burnley. The Townley papers are preserved in the British Museum,
London. For Maria Cosway's quote about her husband, see Hazlitt 1822 and 1826.

6 MS [Eng.] L.961–1953, National Art Library, Victoria and Albert Museum, London.

7 MS Inventory, Fondazione Cosway, Lodi; see also Lloyd 2004.

8 *Madame du Barry* is in the National Gallery of Victoria, Melbourne.

9 Hickey 1923–5, II, pp.362–3.

10 Both drawings are in the Royal Collection.

11 The pendant drawings of Richard and Maria Cosway are in the Fondazione Cosway,
Lodi, while the other self-portrait is in a private collection.

12 Both *Rinaldo and Armida* and *Perseus and Medusa* are in the Graphische Sammlung
Albertina, Vienna. The oil of *Rinaldo and Armida* is in a private collection. Cosway's
copy of Stapylton's translation of Musaeus's epic poem is in the Fondazione
Cosway, Lodi. The three listed drawings from the *Hero and Leander* series are in the

Ashmolean Museum in Oxford, the British Museum in London, and a private collection. *The Death of Leonardo* is also in a private collection.

13 Lawrence MSS, LAW/1/289, Royal Academy, London.

14 *King James VI and I* is in Birmingham Museums and Art Gallery; *The Rape of Ganymede* is in a private collection, as are the *View of the Escorial* and Sebastiano del Piombo's *An Unknown Lady*.

15 *A Franciscan Friar* is in the National Gallery, London; the *Mountainous Landscape* is in the Galleria degli Uffizi, Florence; the *Study after Leonardo's 'Last Supper'* is in the British Museum, London; the sketch of Jan Six is in a private collection; and *The Mass of St Giles* is in the National Gallery, London.

16 The 'Cosway Salt' is in the British Museum, London; for the description of Stratford Place, see Smith 1828, II, pp.401–2.

17 Hazlitt 1930–4, XII, pp.95–6.

18 *The Orléans Children* is in the Musée Condé, Chantilly; the four tapestry cartoons are in the Musée du Louvre, Paris.

19 *General Pasquale Paoli* is in the Galleria Palatina, Palazzo Pitti, Florence; the studies of *Louisa Cosway* are in the Fondazione Cosway, Lodi.

20 *Louisa Cosway on her deathbed* is in the Fondazione Cosway, Lodi.

21 Cosway's library was auctioned at Stanley's, London, 8–12 June 1821. *The Self-portrait as Esau* is in the Galleria degli Uffizi, Florence.

22 The Radnor account book and the portraits are in a private collection.

23 The accounts and the paintings listed are at Powderham Castle, Exeter. The oil portrait of Lord Courtenay was engraved in mezzotint by C. Turner in 1809.

24 The two oil portraits are at Blenheim Palace, Woodstock.

25 This marble memorial is still *in situ*.

26 Christie's, London, 24–27 June 1935.

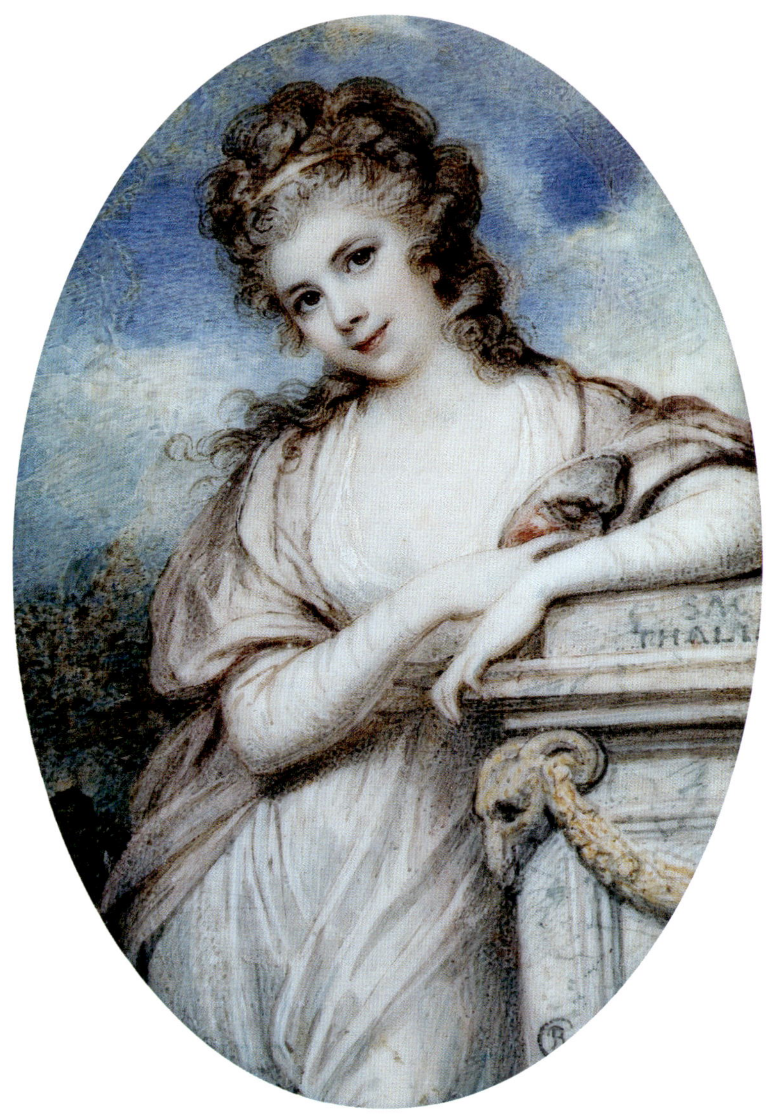
SAC
THALIA

THE COSWAY MINIATURES

1a,b *Thomas Cosway and Katharine Proby, Mrs Thomas Cosway*

Both *c.*1761, 3.2 cm and 3.4 cm
Private Collection
Ref: Edinburgh and London 1995–6, p.114, nos.12 and 13, and p.25, col. pls.4 and 6

Thomas Cosway, who was either an uncle or a cousin of the artist, was a
naval officer based at Portsmouth. In 1761 he married as his second wife
Katharine Proby, and it was then that he most probably commissioned
this pair of miniatures, which still belong to the sitters' descendants.
These portraits are two of Cosway's earliest surviving works, and are
typical of the closely painted 'modest school' style prevalent during the
1760s. The artist painted two other portraits of Thomas Cosway in naval
dress: a head-and-shoulders oil on canvas (Private Collection) and a
three-quarter-length miniature, which is signed and dated 1760 on the
front (sold at Sotheby's, London, 20 July 1981, lot 137).

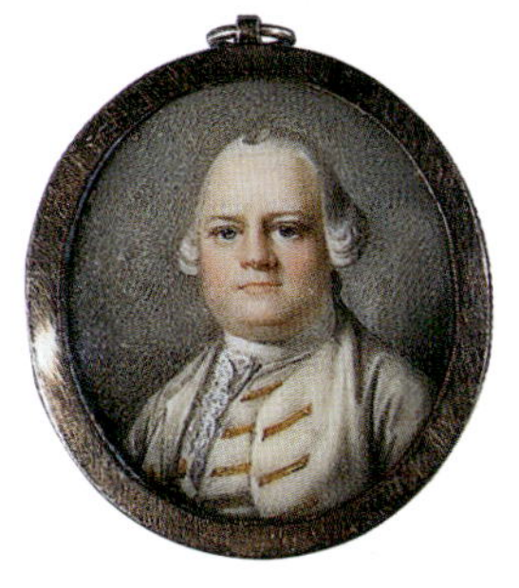
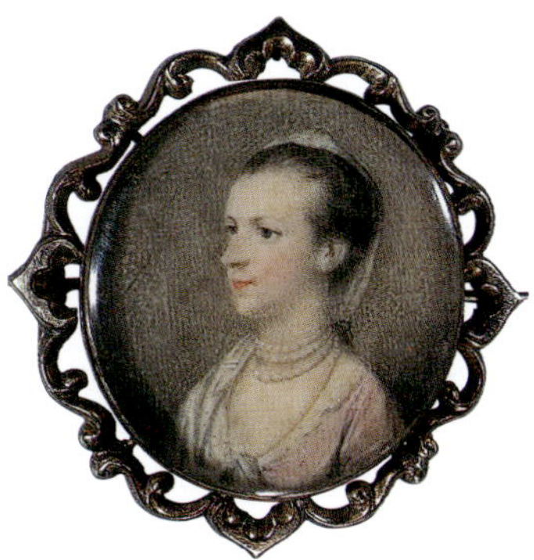

2 *The Hon. Campbell Scott*

c.1766–7, 8.5 cm
The Duke of Buccleuch and Queensberry KT
Ref: Edinburgh 1996–7, p.95, no.69, ill.; *Oxford* DNB 2004

The Hon. Campbell Scott (1747–66), who was a younger brother of
Henry, 3rd Duke of Buccleuch, was the son of Francis, Earl of Dalkeith,
and his wife Caroline, Baroness Greenwich, eldest daughter of the 2nd
Duke of Argyll. An oil portrait of two boys, which was painted by Sir
Joshua Reynolds in 1758, had previously been partially copied by Cosway
in a signed and dated miniature from 1764 (Buccleuch Collection). This
larger miniature of the younger Scott brother was copied by Cosway
from an oil painting by the French master Jean-Baptiste Greuze (Private
Collection). This copy was most likely to have been commissioned by the
family as a memorial, after the sitter had died unexpectedly young in Paris;
the two brothers had been in Paris as part of the Grand Tour and were
being tutored there by Adam Smith, the celebrated moral philosopher
and political economist. This densely painted miniature is notable for its
unusually large size and for the rare instance of the artist signing his name
in full on the front of the work.

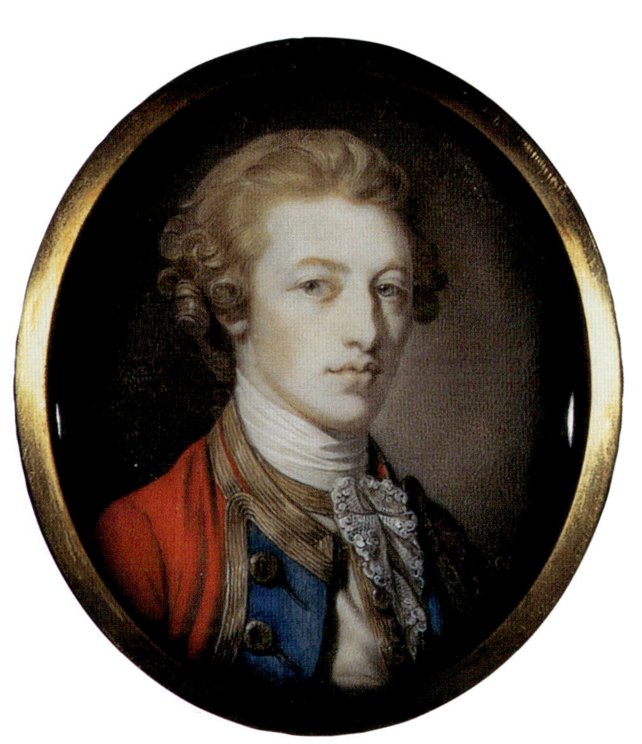

3 *Miss Elliot in the character of Pallas or Minerva*

1769, 11.2 cm
Fondazione Cosway, Lodi
Ref: Edinburgh and London 1995–6, p.114, no.17, and p.25, col. pl.5; *Oxford* DNB 2004

Ann Elliot (1743–69), a courtesan and noted comic actress, was portrayed
in the last year of her life by Cosway in an untraced half-length oil
portrait as well as in this ambitious large miniature, which was retained
by the artist for his own collection. This theatrically posed composition,
which is redolent of Italian baroque painting, was initially exhibited in
London at the Society of Artists during 1769 as 'A portrait in miniature
of a Lady as Pallas'. Cosway's related oil was shown the following year at
the Royal Academy as 'A portrait in the character of Minerva'. One or
other of these two versions was engraved in mezzotint by J. Saunders
and published in 1772 as 'Miss Elliot in the character of Minerva'.

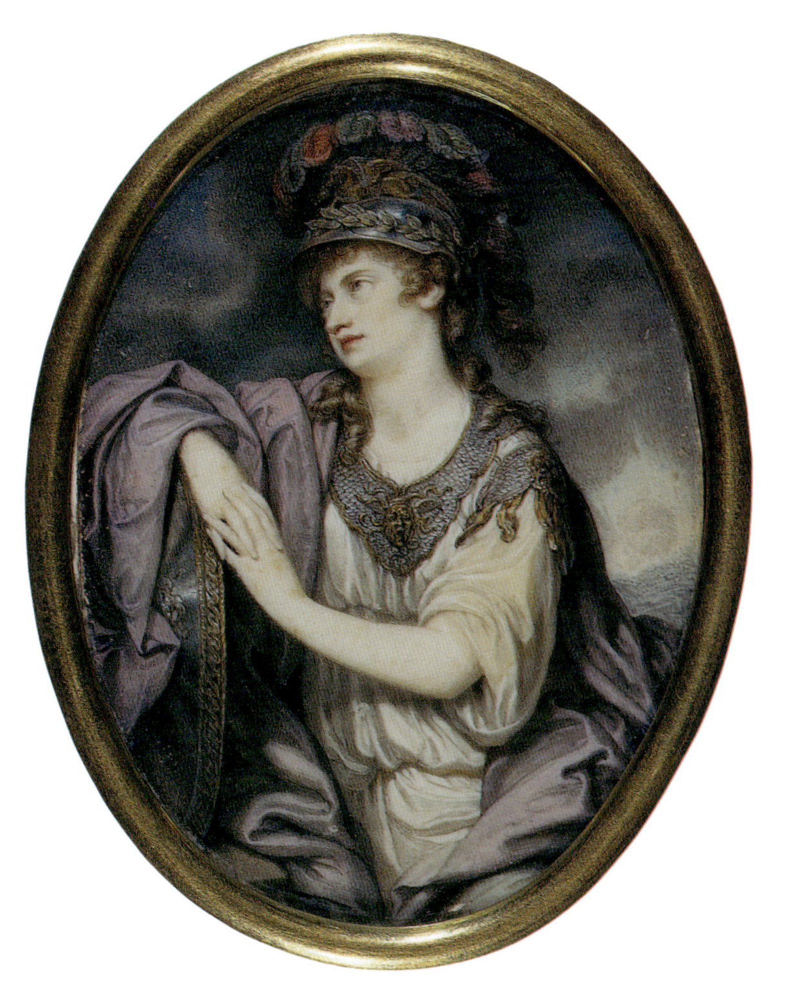

4 *Self-portrait in profile*

*c.*1770, 5 cm
The Metropolitan Museum of Art, New York (Gift of Miss Charlotte Guilford Mulhofer, 1962).
Photograph © 1994 The Metropolitan Museum of Art
Refs: Edinburgh and London 1995–6, p.114, no.18 and p.27, col. pl.17; New York 1996,
pp.131–2, no.130 and p.46, col. pl. and col. frontispiece; *Oxford DNB* 2004

In this early profile self-portrait Cosway can be seen emulating the closely
painted technique and style of the German-born Jeremiah Meyer
(1735–89), who at that time was the leading miniaturist in London. In
this tour de force of miniature painting Cosway presented his distinctive
simian features in the guise of one of the supremely fashionable
'macaronies' or dandies, who were frequently caricatured during the early
1770s. Cosway, who was short in height, was himself the subject of two
satirical prints from 1772: Matthew Darly etched *The miniature macaroni*,
while Philip Dawe engraved in mezzotint *The macaroni painter, or Billy
Dimple sitting for his picture.*

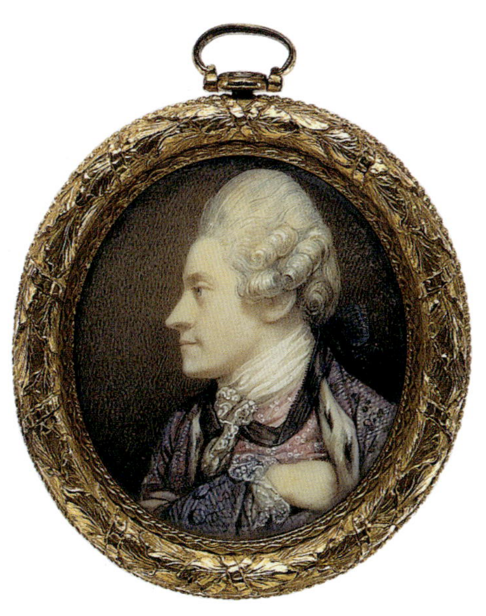

5a,b *Thomas, 2nd Baron Lyttelton* [verso and recto]

c.1772 (setting *c*.1779), 4.4 cm
Private Collection
Ref: Edinburgh and London 1995–6, p.115, no.20, and p.27, col. pl.15 (recto only);
Oxford DNB 2004

Thomas, 2nd Baron Lyttelton (1744–79), who succeeded his father in
1773, was a politician and one of the most notorious libertines of the
1770s. Cosway probably painted this miniature in 1772, the year of
Lyttelton's short-lived marriage to the wealthy young East India
Company widow Apphia Peach (née Witts). The miniature's lavish setting
in gold, enamel and diamonds was likely to have been commissioned
from the leading London-based jeweller James Morisset by Lyttelton's
family after his strange early death. Bizarrely, and correctly as it turned
out, Lord Lyttelton had told his friends that a ghostly woman had
appeared before him, first disguised as a robin, and had predicted his
death within three days. Cosway posthumously portrayed Lyttelton and
his dramatic demise in an untraced half-length oil painting of 1780,
which was engraved in mezzotint the following year by C. Townley.

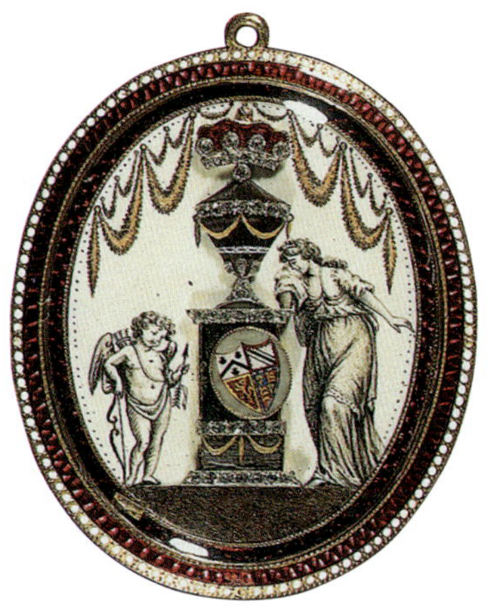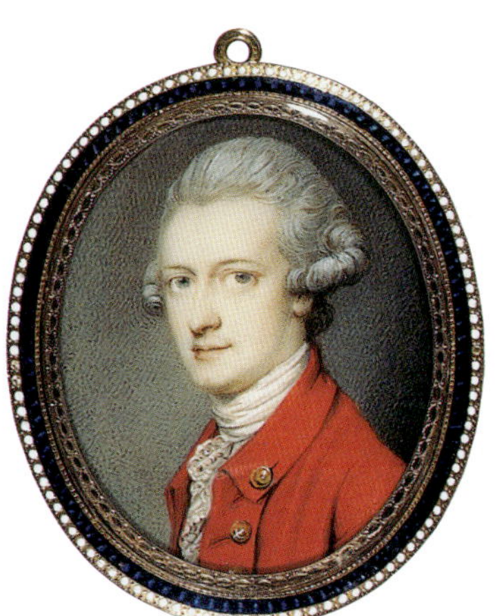

6 *Robert, 4th Duke of Ancaster and Kesteven*

*c.*1778–9, 3.2 cm (box: 12.1 cm wide)
Private Collection
Ref: Edinburgh and London 1995–6, p.115, no.21 and p.27, col. pl.18

Robert Bertie (1756–79) succeeded his father in 1778 as 20th Baron Willoughby de Eresby and 4th Duke of Ancaster and Kesteven. Having served as an aide-de-camp to General Clinton in the American War of Independence, he died unmarried soon after his return to Britain. The dukedom passed to an uncle, while the barony of Willoughby de Eresby passed to his eldest sister, Lady Priscilla Bertie. The unusually lavish setting for Cosway's miniature is comprised of diamonds within a silver frame, surrounded with the duke's plaited hair under glass. This arrangement in turn forms the lid of a shuttle-shaped patch-box made of gold.

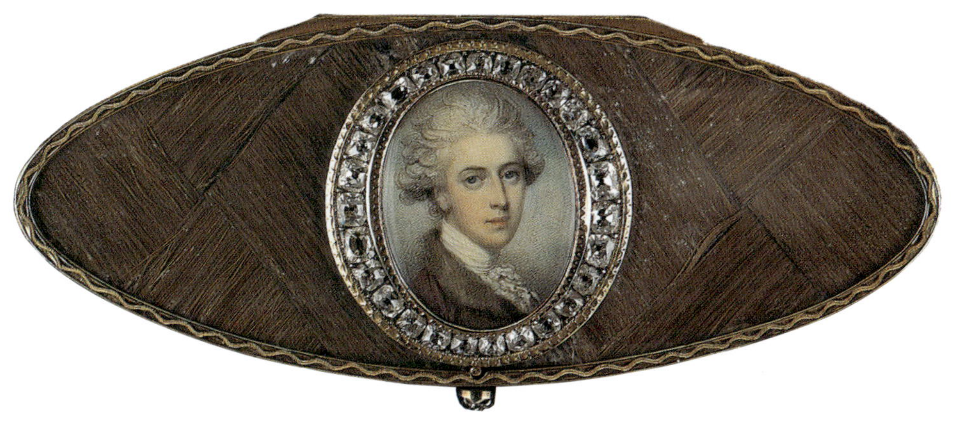

7 *The Ladies Priscilla and Georgiana Bertie* ('The Ancaster Box')

*c.*1780, 4.8 cm (box: 11.7 cm wide)
Private Collection
Ref: Edinburgh and London 1995–6, p.117, no.47, and p.36, col.pl.22a

This outstanding ivory and gold patch-box was likely to have been commissioned by or for Mary Panton, Duchess of Ancaster (1725–93), whose profile miniature portrait by an unknown artist is set into the base of this box. Inside the lid is a miniature after Cosway of her recently deceased son, Robert, 4th Duke of Ancaster (1756–79). On top of the lid is an elegant double portrait miniature by Cosway of the late duke's two sisters, the Ladies Priscilla and Georgiana Bertie. In 1779 the older sister married Sir Peter Burrell, later 1st Baron Gwydir, and the following year she became the Baroness Willoughby de Eresby in her own right. In 1791 the younger sister married George, 1st Marquess of Cholmondeley.

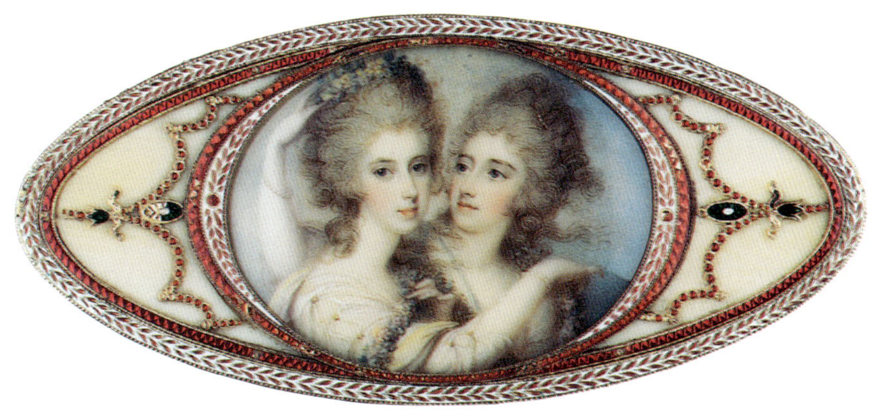

8 *The Hon. Francis Charteris of Amisfield* (later 7th Earl of Wemyss)

1779 (setting 1787), 4.3 cm
The Earl of Wemyss & March, KT
Ref: Edinburgh 1999, p.58, no.30, and p.13, fig.4

The Hon. Francis Charteris of Amisfield (1725–1808) became the 7th Earl
of Wemyss in 1787, when it was likely that this splendid diamond and
enamelled setting was added to Cosway's earlier miniature. The seventh
earl's account book records that this portrait originally had a gold setting,
both it and the miniature by Cosway costing the sitter seventeen guineas
in 1779. Eight years earlier in 1771 this Scottish peer, whose principal
estate was near Haddington in East Lothian, had sat for a modest portrait
from Ozias Humphry (1742–1810), one of Cosway's main rivals as a
miniaturist, which had cost the sitter twelve guineas (Private Collection).

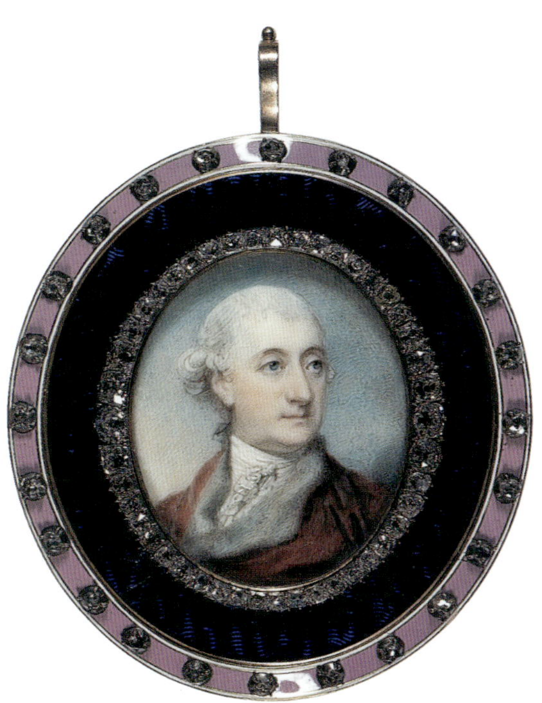

9 *The Prince of Wales* (later the Prince Regent and George IV)

1782, 9.8 cm
National Portrait Gallery, London
Refs: Edinburgh and London 1995–6, p.117, no.49 and p.58, col. pl.51; Lloyd 2004,
pp.196 and 205, fig.92; *Oxford DNB* 2004

The eighteen-year-old Prince of Wales first sat to Cosway in 1780 for five
miniatures. Two years later the prince was portrayed by his favourite
miniaturist in this colourful and flamboyant example, for which the artist
charged twenty guineas. This particular work may have been intended as
a gift for the prince's then mistress, the actress Mrs 'Perdita' Robinson
(1758–1800), as it is known that she sat to Cosway that year at the behest
of the prince for a miniature and a portrait drawing. In this dashing and
somewhat effeminate portrayal the prince is shown with a jauntily
angled hat and wearing the star of the Order of the Garter on a striking
red coat.

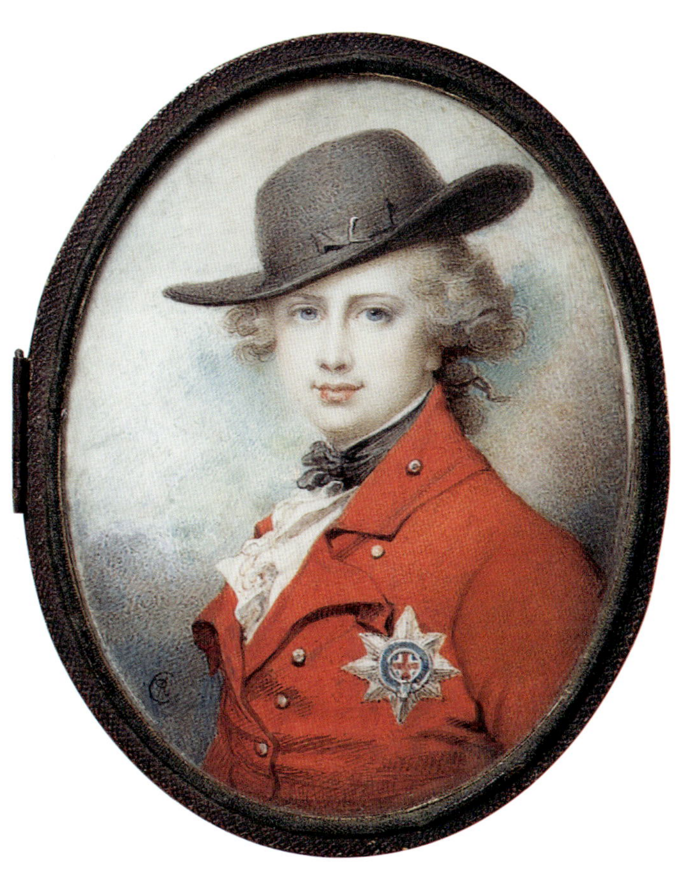

10 *Mrs Abington as Thalia or the Comic Muse*

*c.*1783, 14.5 cm
The Trustees of the Bowood Collection
Ref: Edinburgh and London 1995–6, p.118, no.56 and p.60, col. pl.55; *Oxford DNB* 2004

Frances or Fanny Barton (1737–1815), who grew up in poverty and married the trumpeter James Abington in 1759, was one of the foremost comic actresses of her generation. The mood, pose and composition of Cosway's unusually large miniature were inspired by Sir Joshua Reynolds's full-length oil portrait of the sitter as Thalia or the Comic Muse (National Trust, Waddesdon Manor), which had been completed two decades earlier. Cosway also produced a full-length portrait drawing of Mrs Abington dancing and placing a wreath on a bust of Shakespeare (Waddesdon Manor), which was engraved in stipple by F. Bartolozzi in 1783. A related but less finished study by Cosway for this drawing also survives (Fogg Art Museum, Cambridge, Massachusetts).

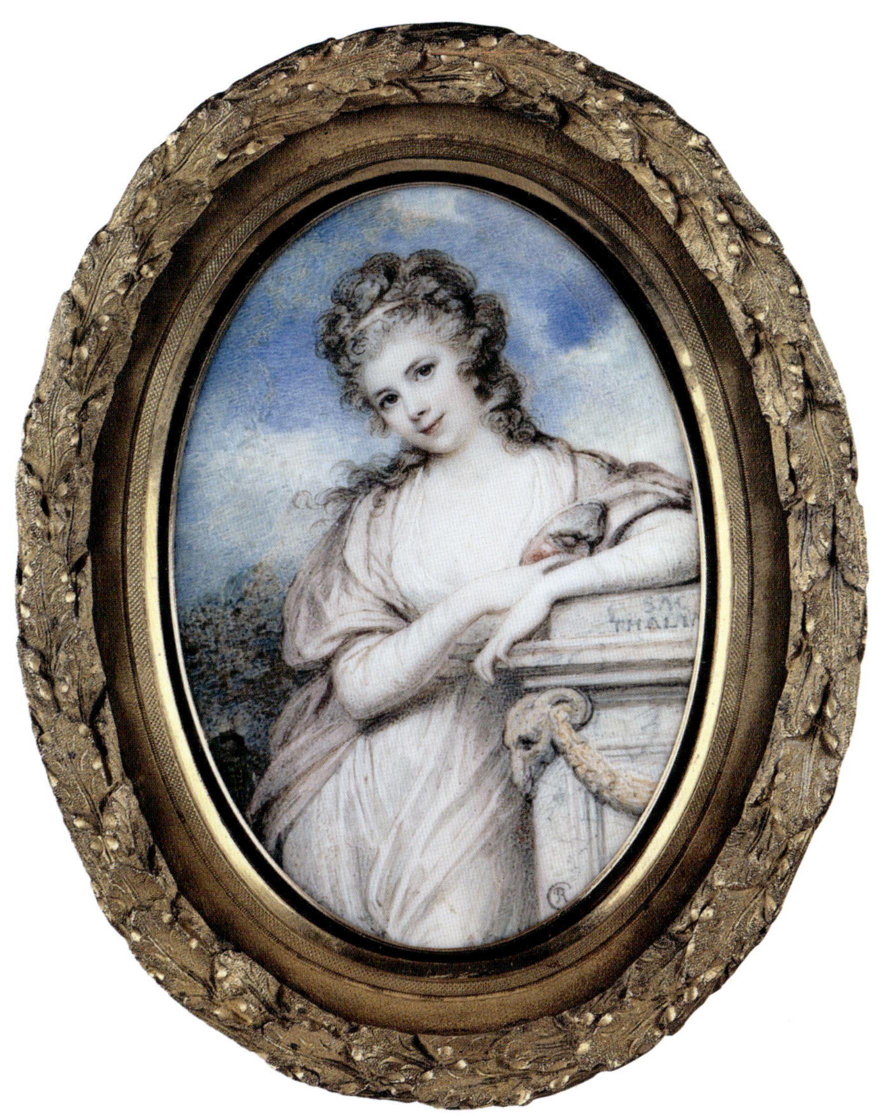

SAC
THALIÆ

11 *Anne Seymour Damer*

1785, 6.1 cm
National Portrait Gallery, London
Ref: Edinburgh and London 1995–6, p.118, no.57, and p.61, col. pl. 58; *Oxford DNB* 2004

The Hon. Anne Conway (1748–1826), who was the only child of the
politician the Hon. Henry Seymour Conway and his wife Caroline Bruce,
daughter of the 4th Duke of Argyll, married the Hon. John Damer in
1767. She was an accomplished author and versatile sculptor, known for
her neoclassical statuary in terracotta, marble and bronze. As a friend,
executor and residuary legatee of the noted antiquarian Horace Walpole,
she inherited his famous neo-Gothic villa of Strawberry Hill in
Twickenham, together with most of its contents. Among these was a full-
length portrait drawing by Cosway of Mrs Damer, depicted resting while
carving a marble bust of Paris (Private Collection). In this miniature
Cosway portrayed Mrs Damer in Elizabethan fancy dress, which may
have been intended to echo the image of Mary, Queen of Scots. The front
of the miniature bears a rare instance of a monogrammed signature,
while on the back is one of the earliest instances of Cosway's florid Latin
signature as Primarius Pictor, which the Prince of Wales permitted the
artist to use from 1785.

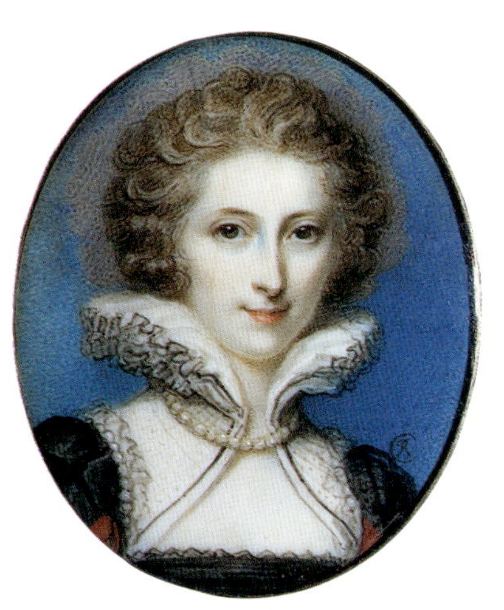

12 *Georgiana, Duchess of Devonshire*

1786, 8.9 cm
© The Devonshire Collection, Chatsworth.
Reproduced by permission of the Chatsworth Settlement Trustees.
Refs: Edinburgh and London 1995–6, p.120, no.76, and p.62, col. pl.61; Lloyd 2004,
pp.195 and 205, fig.91; *Oxford DNB* 2004

Lady Georgiana Spencer (1757–1806), who married the 5th Duke of
Devonshire in 1774, was a leading figure in fashionable Whig society
during the late eighteenth century. She was Cosway's earliest major
patron, commissioning just over £300 worth of miniatures – including
nine of herself, from the artist between 1776 and 1789. For this dazzling
large miniature Cosway charged the duchess £36 in 1786. Throughout the
1770s and during the early 1780s Cosway was living at 4 Berkeley Street
or Row, immediately behind Devonshire House on Piccadilly. It is likely
that Cosway's commissions from this influential aristocratic neighbour
facilitated the artist's introduction in 1780 to her friend the Prince of Wales,
who in turn was to become Cosway's principal patron.

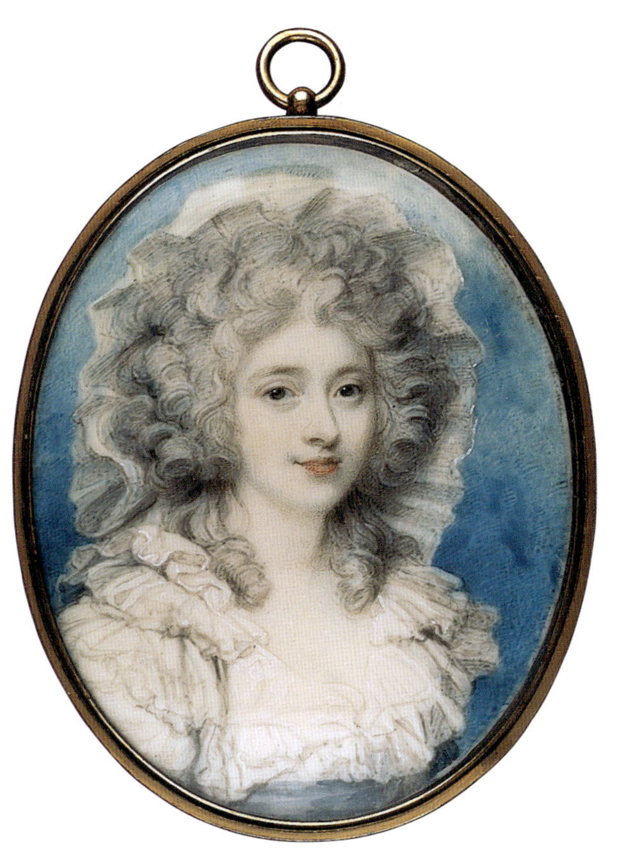

13a,b *Mrs Fitzherbert and her Eye*

1786, 3.2 cm and 8.3 cm
Private collection
Ref: Edinburgh and London 1995–6, p.118, nos.59–60 and p.59, col. pls.52 and 54; Lloyd
2004, pp.196 and 206, figs.95–6; *Oxford DNB* 2004

Maria Anne Smythe (1756–1837) was the eldest daughter of Walter and
Mary Smythe of Acton Burnell in Shropshire, who were a Roman
Catholic family. She was married first in 1775 to Edward Weld of
Lulworth Castle in Dorset, and then in 1778 to Thomas Fitzherbert of
Swynnerton in Shropshire. Twice widowed before she was twenty-five, in
1785 she secretly (and morganatically) married George, Prince of Wales.
It was in the previous year that she had first sat to Cosway for the prince.
This portrait, which is surrounded by her plaited hair, and the related
miniature of her eye were commissioned from Cosway in 1786 at a cost
of thirty and five guineas respectively. The prince always wore one of
Cosway's miniatures of Mrs Fitzherbert in a diamond locket around his
neck under his shirt, and he was buried with it on his body at St George's
Chapel, Windsor Castle, in 1830.

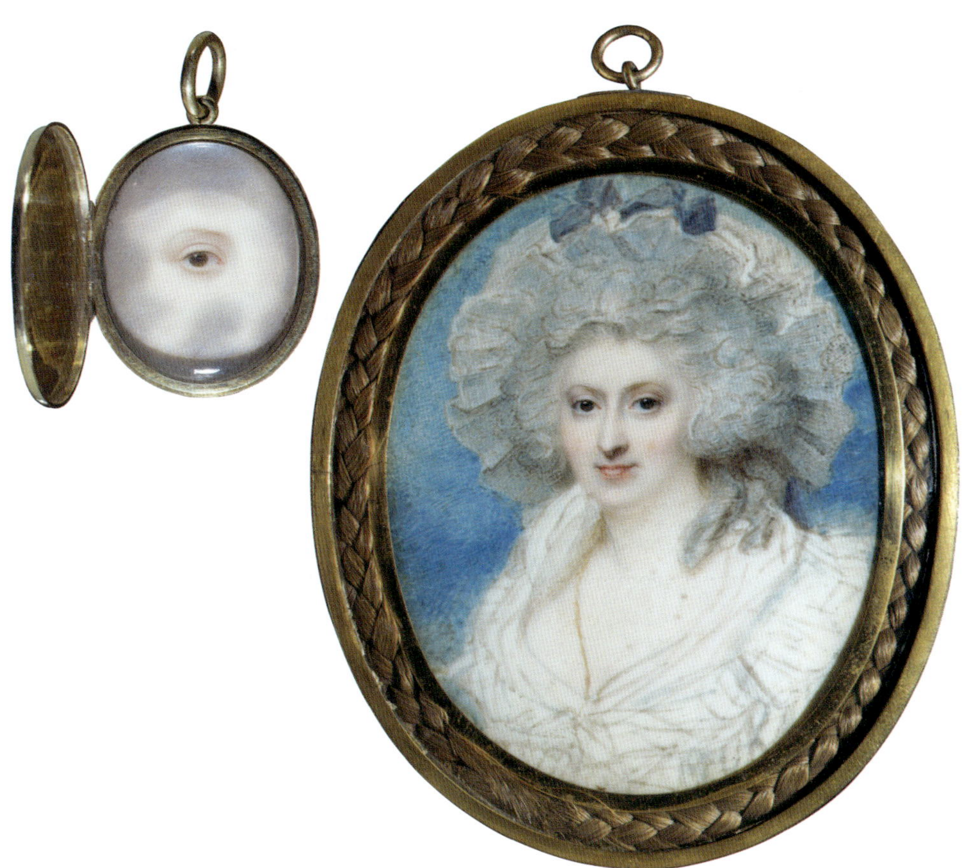

14 *Warren Hastings*

1787, 5.7 cm
National Portrait Gallery, London
Ref: Edinburgh and London 1995–6, p.119, no.65, and p.63, col. pl.65; *Oxford DNB* 2004

Warren Hastings (1732–1818) was Governor-General of Bengal and the architect of the future British Empire in India. One of the most controversial men of his time, he frequently sat for his portrait. According to a letter in 1787 from Maria Cosway to her lover Thomas Jefferson, then the American ambassador in Paris, Hastings's sitting to Richard Cosway for his miniature took place 'as Mr H was at the very moment the trial was going on'. This was just when Burke and Sheridan were making their opening speeches against Hastings at the start of his seven-year trial for impeachment over alleged corruption in India. In this portrait Cosway successfully caught a look of stoic determination in Hastings's appearance.

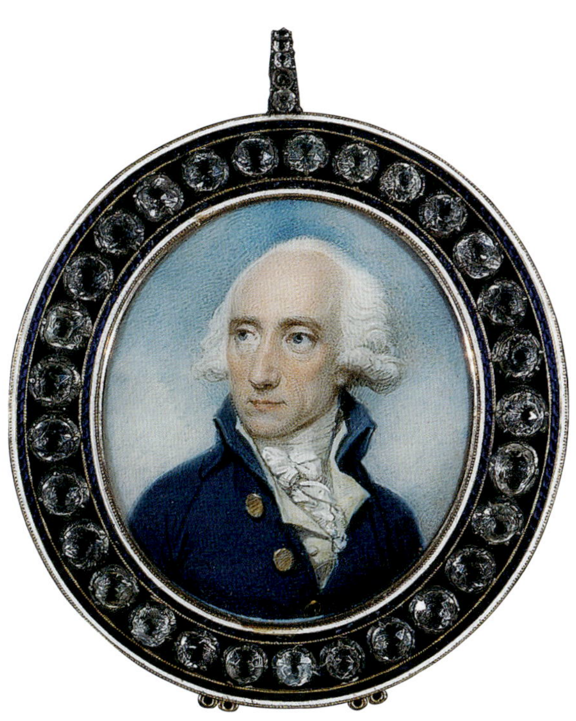

15 *Margaret Cocks* (later Mrs Joseph Smith)

1787, 7.2 cm
V&A Images, Victoria and Albert Museum, London
Ref: Edinburgh and London 1995–6, p.119, no.63 and p.61, col. pl.59; Asleson and Bennett
2001, pp.72–5; Bryant 2003, pp.364–7, fig.1

Margaret Cocks (1773–1847) was the second daughter of Joseph Cocks, a
barrister-at-law, and of his wife Margaret. A wealthy heiress, in 1798 she
became the second wife of Joseph Smith, who was secretary to William
Pitt the Younger. Cosway, in an unusual composition for one of his
miniatures, has shown the teenaged sitter in profile, mourning before a
neoclassical urn containing the remains of her elder sister, Mary, Mrs
Henry Russell, who had died in 1786, as revealed by the monogram and
date inscribed on the urn. This portrait is signed in full and dated by the
artist on the back. The miniature was formerly thought to represent the
sitter's niece, Mary Russell (d.1856), who later married the Revd Henry
Domvile, and who was painted by Reynolds in a double portrait with her
aunt in 1789–90 (Iveagh Bequest, Kenwood House, London). Cosway
also portrayed Margaret Cocks in 1787 in a three-quarter-length oil
portrait, where she is shown grieving on reading a letter with the news of
the death of her sister, whose miniature she is wearing (Huntington
Library and Art Collections, San Marino, California).

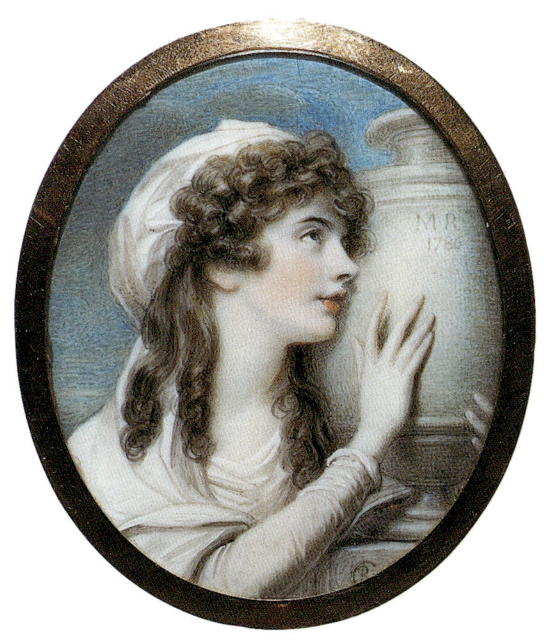

16 *Unknown Lady* (formerly entitled *Mrs Fitzherbert*)

*c.*1790, 7.2 cm high
Reproduced by kind permission of the Trustees of the Wallace Collection, London
Ref: Reynolds 1980, pp.178–9, no.149, ill. and p.18, col. pl.IIa

This masterpiece by Cosway in the art of miniature painting on ivory was
long thought to represent Mrs Fitzherbert, the morganatic wife of
George, Prince of Wales. However, comparison with other known
Cosway miniatures of Mrs Fitzherbert categorically rules out such an
identification. An inscription scratched inside the original gilt-metal frame
bears the date 1790. If this date is correct, the miniature could possibly be
a portrait of Maria Cosway, who was well known for wearing a turban.
This work is notable for the intense engagement of the sitter with the
artist, the effect of which is partially achieved through the direct gaze and
the strongly angled head

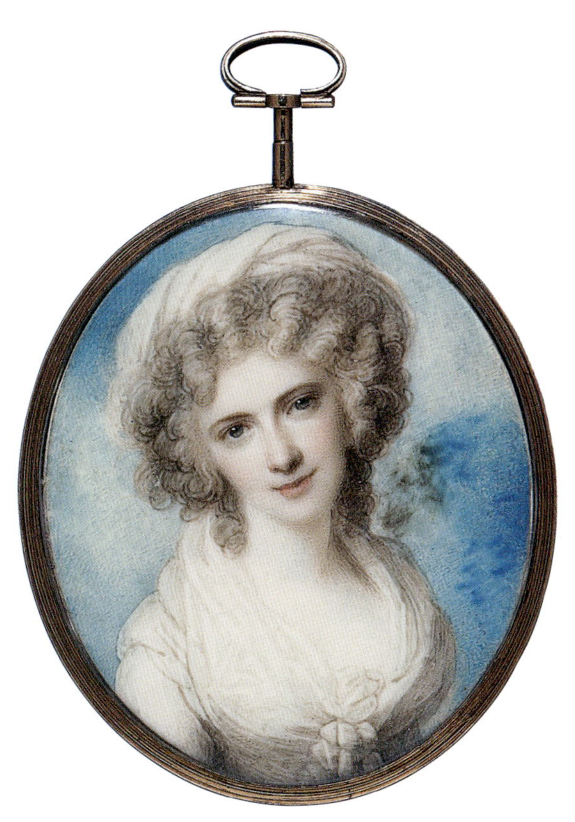

17 *Lady Elizabeth Foster* (later Duchess of Devonshire)

*c.*1790, 7.7 cm
National Gallery of Victoria, Melbourne (Felton Bequest)
Ref: Williamson 1906–8, II, p.59, no.278, pl.LXXXVI(2); Melbourne 1983, pp.48–9,
col. pl.c; *Oxford DNB* 2004

Lady Elizabeth Foster (1757–1824) was the daughter of Frederick, 4th
Earl of Bristol, the famous Italophile 'Bishop-Earl' and his wife Elizabeth
Davers. After the death of her first husband John Thomas Foster in 1782,
she became a particularly close friend of Georgiana, Duchess of
Devonshire, as well as mistress of her husband William, the 5th Duke, in
the most notorious *ménage à trois* of the Regency period. After the death
of Georgiana in 1806, Lady Elizabeth Foster became the second wife of
the duke in 1809, although he died only two years later. In 1816 she
moved to Rome, where she died. This miniature is set in its original gold
frame, surrounded with blue enamel and set with pearls. Another similar
miniature by Cosway of this sitter, signed and dated 1790, was sold at
auction recently (Sotheby's, London, 6 March 2003, lot 10).

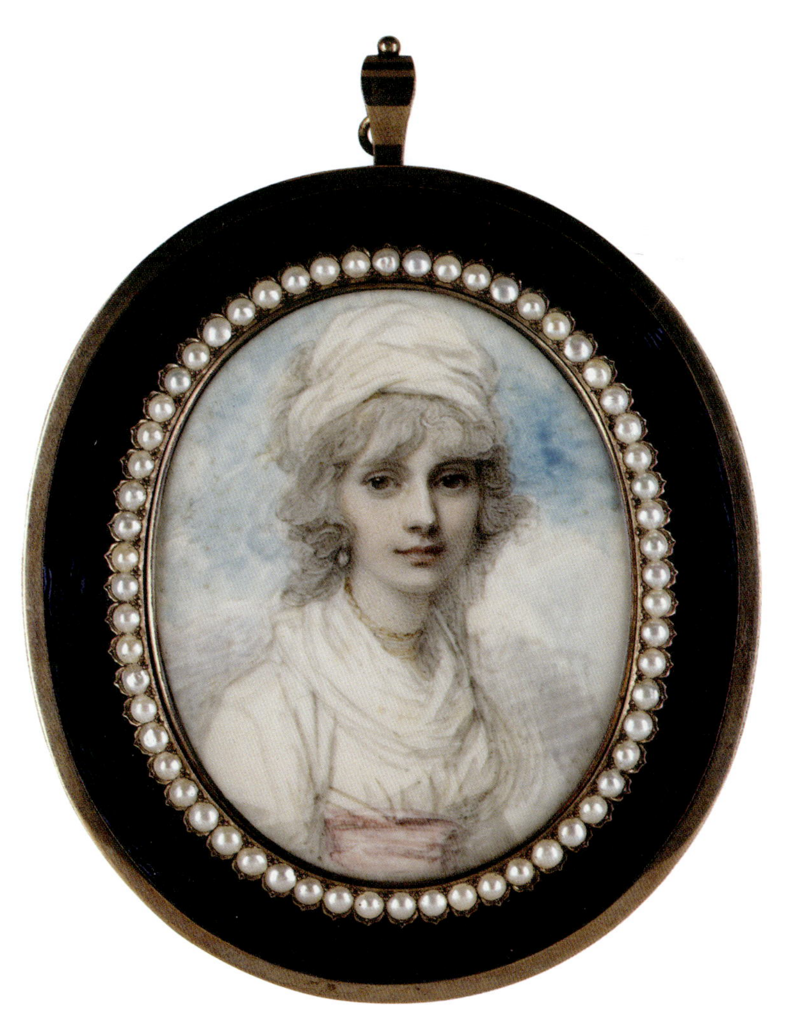

18 *James, 3rd Earl of Hopetoun*

1789, 7.9 cm
Yale Center for British Art, New Haven (Paul Mellon Collection)
Refs: Edinburgh and London 1995–6, p.119, no.67 and p.61, col.pl.57; Lloyd 2004,
pp.198 and 208, fig.116; *Oxford DNB* 2004

James Hope-Johnstone (1741–1816), who was the second son of John,
2nd Earl of Hopetoun and his first wife Anne Ogilvy, succeeded his
father in 1781 as 3rd Earl of Hopetoun and was *de jure* 5th Earl of
Annandale and Hartfell. He served as a Scottish representative peer from
1784 to 1790, and was appointed Lord Lieutenant of Linlithgowshire
from 1794 until his death. Lord Hopetoun sat to Cosway for his miniature
twice in 1789, for which the artist charged thirty guineas a piece.
Likewise his wife Lady Elizabeth Carnegie sat to Cosway for miniatures
in 1789 and 1792. The second pair of miniatures were sold privately on
the London art market during the 1970s. Both of the miniatures in this
pair are signed in full and dated on the back.

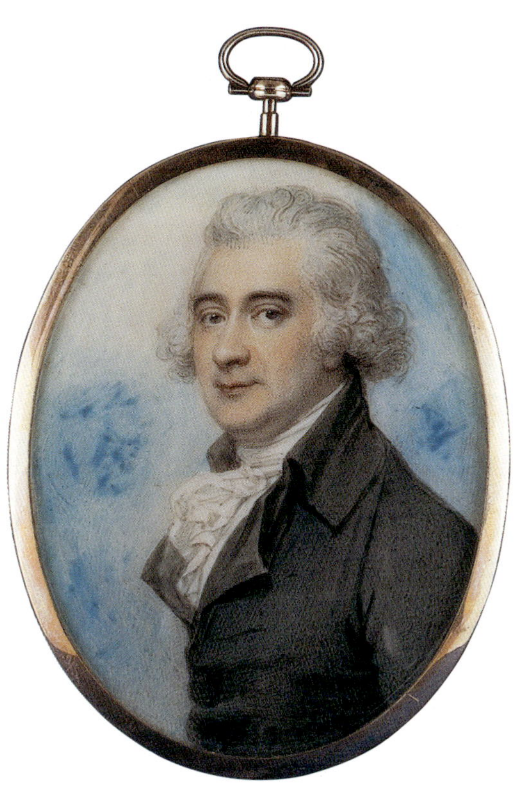

19 *Elizabeth, Countess of Hopetoun*

1789, 7.6 cm
Yale Center for British Art, New Haven (Paul Mellon Collection)
Refs: Edinburgh and London 1995–6, p.119, no.68 and p.61, col. pl.56; Lloyd 2004,
pp.198 and 208, fig.115; *Oxford DNB* 2004

Lady Elizabeth Carnegie (1750–93), who was the daughter of George, 6th
Earl of Northesk, married James Hope, 3rd Earl of Hopetoun in 1766.
Together they had six daughters. The black ribbon attached to her dress
in Cosway's sensitively painted miniature may refer to the death of one
of her children. Lady Hopetoun was also portrayed by Cosway at this
date in a full-length drawing, together with two of her daughters
(National Gallery of Scotland, Edinburgh). In 1787 another oil portrait of
her by Gainsborough was described by the writer Sir Henry Bate: 'her
ladyship, though not in the full bloom of life, possesses that elegance,
grace and beauty, which form the best combination a picture can have'.

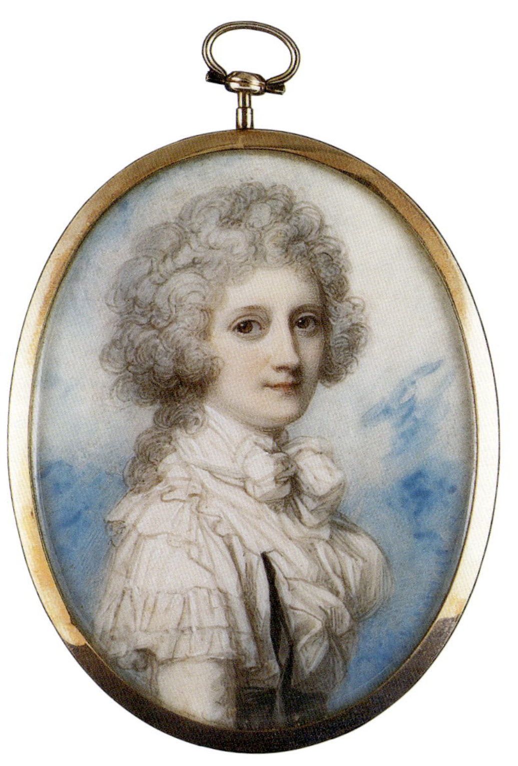

20 *The Duke of Clarence* (later William IV)

1789, 7.8 cm
Lt.-Col. R. L. Jenkins (on loan to the National Portrait Gallery, London)
Refs: Edinburgh and London 1995–6, p.119, no.69 and p.63, col. pl.62; Lloyd 2004,
pp.199 and 208, fig.122; *Oxford DNB* 2004

The Duke of Clarence, later William IV (1765–1837), was the second son
of George III and Queen Charlotte. After the Prince of Wales, his older
brother, the Duke of Clarence was the most significant patron of Cosway
from within the royal family. In 1789 he sat to the artist for six miniatures,
including three smaller works priced at twenty guineas, and three larger
examples costing thirty guineas each. Two years later, in 1791, the duke
sat to Cosway for five more larger miniatures, two of which are still in the
Royal Collection. This portrait was probably presented by the Duke of
Clarence to Sally, the daughter of George Winne, the Mayor of Plymouth
in 1788, after they had met at a ball there the previous year and
corresponded for two years. The miniature has remained in the possession
of the sitter's descendants to the present day.

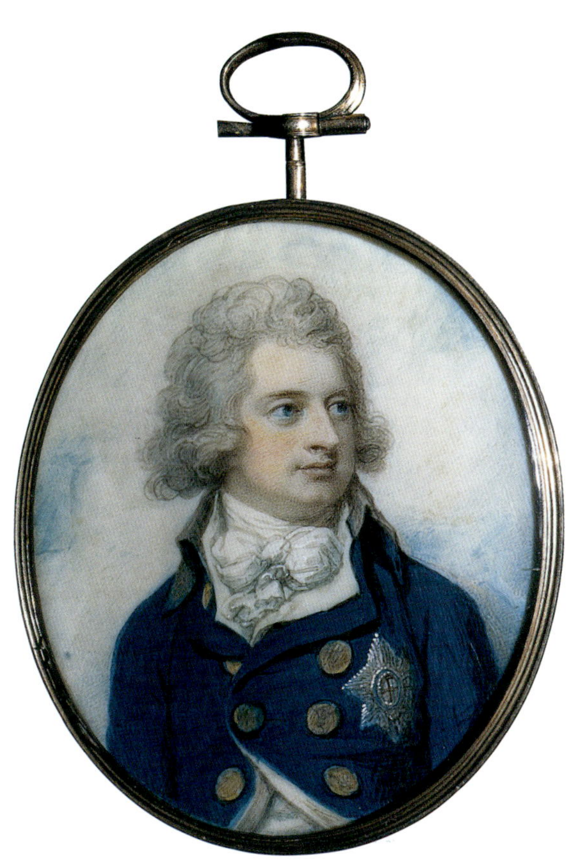

21 *The Prince of Wales* (later the Prince Regent and George IV)

1792, 8.1 cm
National Portrait Gallery, London
Ref: Edinburgh and London 1995–6, p.124, no.118 and p.58, col. pl.50; Lloyd 2004,
pp.197 and 206, fig.99; *Oxford DNB* 2004

In 1792 the Prince of Wales sat to Cosway for three miniatures, including
one smaller work priced at twenty-five guineas, which was intended for
his private secretary John Willet Payne, and two larger portraits priced at
thirty guineas each. One of those miniatures was intended as a gift for
Mrs Fitzherbert, the prince's morganatic wife, and the other for the
singer Anna Maria Phillips, Mrs Crouch, with whom the prince was having
a short-lived affair. This miniature, which is signed in full and dated on
the back, and set in a lavish closing double locket of gold, may have been
intended by the prince for either of the two women in his life at that
time. Cosway has shown his principal patron wearing the robes, badge
and star of the Order of the Garter in a swaggering image redolent of Van
Dyck's portraiture.

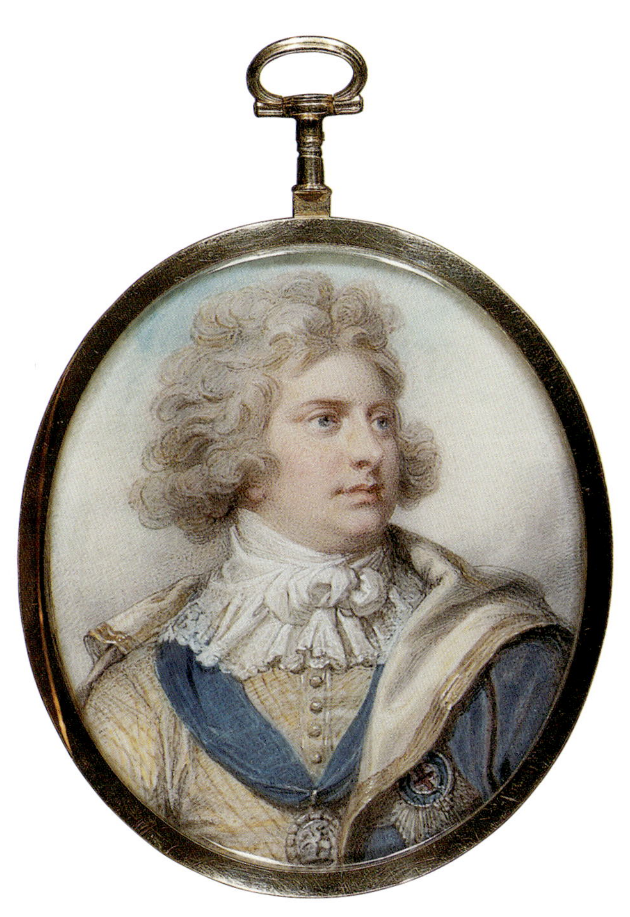

22 *Princess Sophia*

1792, 7.9 cm
The Royal Collection © 2004, Her Majesty Queen Elizabeth II
Refs: Edinburgh and London 1995–6, p.124, no.117; Lloyd 2004, p.197 and 206, fig.101;
Fraser 2004; *Oxford DNB* 2004

Princess Sophia (1777–1848) was the fifth daughter of George III and
Queen Charlotte. Cosway portrayed her, when aged fifteen, for her eldest
brother at a cost of thirty guineas. The favourite sister of the Prince of
Wales, in 1800 she had a child, Thomas, by an older equerry Major-General
Thomas Garth. In later life Princess Sophia suffered from ill health and
was never permitted to marry. This miniature is a typically sensitive
example of Cosway's portrait miniatures of women from the early 1790s.
Here he utilises a very limited palette with light touches of blue in the
sky, while leaving parts of the ivory background unpainted to suggest
white clouds.

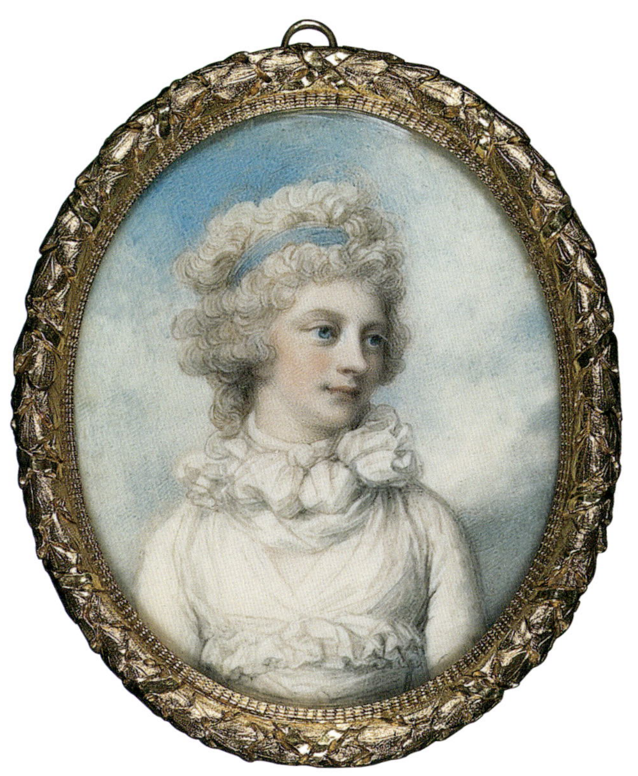

23 *Louisa Paolina Angelica Cosway*

*c.*1792, 6.8 cm high
City Museum and Art Gallery, Plymouth
Refs: Edinburgh and London 1995–6, p.124, no.127 and pp.66 and 70, col. pls.68 and 71

Louisa Paolina Angelica Cosway (1790–6) was the only child of Richard
and Maria Cosway. Born in London on 4 May 1790, she was part named
after her godmother, Princess Louisa of Stolberg, Countess of Albany, the
former wife of Prince Charles Edward Stuart, and part after her godfather
General Pasquale Paoli, the Corsican patriot exiled in London, and intimate
friend of Maria Cosway. After recovering from a difficult confinement and
birth, Maria travelled to Italy for health reasons, but did not return to
London to see her daughter for another four and a half years. Louisa
died from a fever on 29 July 1796, after catching a sore throat. This
engaging miniature of Louisa by her father demonstrates the artist's
empathy in the portrayal of children.

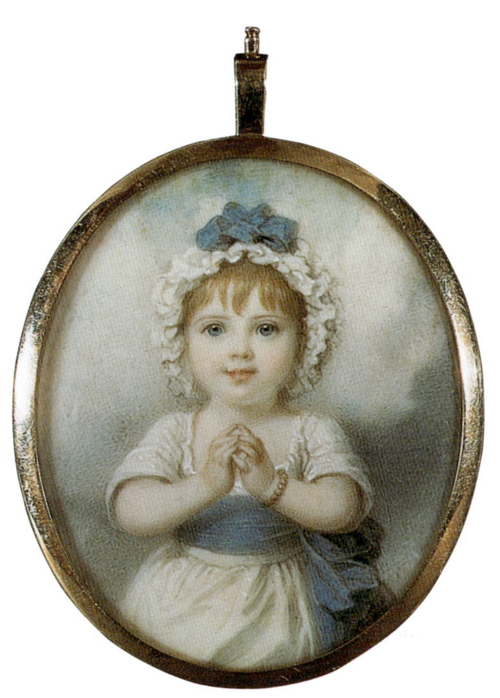

24 *Unknown Lady*
(formerly entitled **Catherine Vesey, Mrs James Fitzgerald**)

1794, 8.3 cm
Huntington Library and Art Collections, San Marino, California
Ref: Edinburgh and London 1995–6, p.124, no.120 and p.86, col. pl.89; *Oxford DNB* 2004

This miniature has traditionally been thought to represent Catherine
Fitzgerald (d.1832), although the erotic nature of the work makes such an
identification unlikely. Catherine Fitzgerald was the youngest daughter of
Revd Henry Vesey, warden of Galway, and his wife Mary Gerry. She
married James Fitzgerald (1742–1835), a noted Irish politician. When he
refused a peerage, she was created Baroness Fitzgerald and Vesey of Clare
and Inchicronan in 1826. Their eldest son, William Vesey Fitzgerald,
succeeded to her Irish peerage in 1832 as Baron Fitzgerald and Vesey.
This miniature, which is fully signed and dated on the back, is one of
Cosway's most alluring portrayals of a female sitter from the 1790s. The
frame of gold and diamonds was probably added at the request of the
dealer Joseph, Lord Duveen, who sold an important group of Cosway
miniatures and drawings to the Californian railroad magnate Henry
Huntington in 1926.

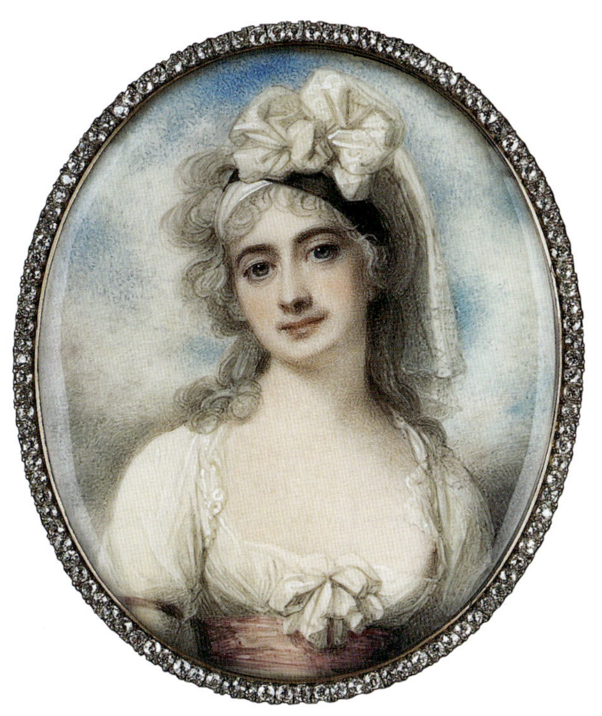

25 *Princess Amelia*

1795, 9 cm
The Royal Collection © 2004, Her Majesty Queen Elizabeth II
Refs: Edinburgh and London 1995–6, p.125, no.130; Lloyd 2004, pp.197 and 207, fig.106;
Fraser 2004; *Oxford DNB* 2004

Princess Amelia (1783–1810) was the youngest and favourite daughter of
George III and Queen Charlotte. She always suffered poor health, and
was diagnosed as having tuberculosis at the age of fifteen. She never
married, despite falling in love at Weymouth in 1801 with one of the
king's equerries, Colonel Thomas Fitzroy, second son of Lord
Southampton. Cosway was commissioned to paint this miniature of the
twelve-year-old princess in 1795 for her eldest brother, the Prince of
Wales, at a cost of thirty guineas. As a child of six, Princess Amelia had
sat to Sir Thomas Lawrence for an oil portrait where she was shown
holding a bunch of roses (Royal Collection). In this miniature Cosway
has echoed that pose but omitted the roses in an exceptionally delicate
example of his 'unfinished' miniature painting style from the 1790s.

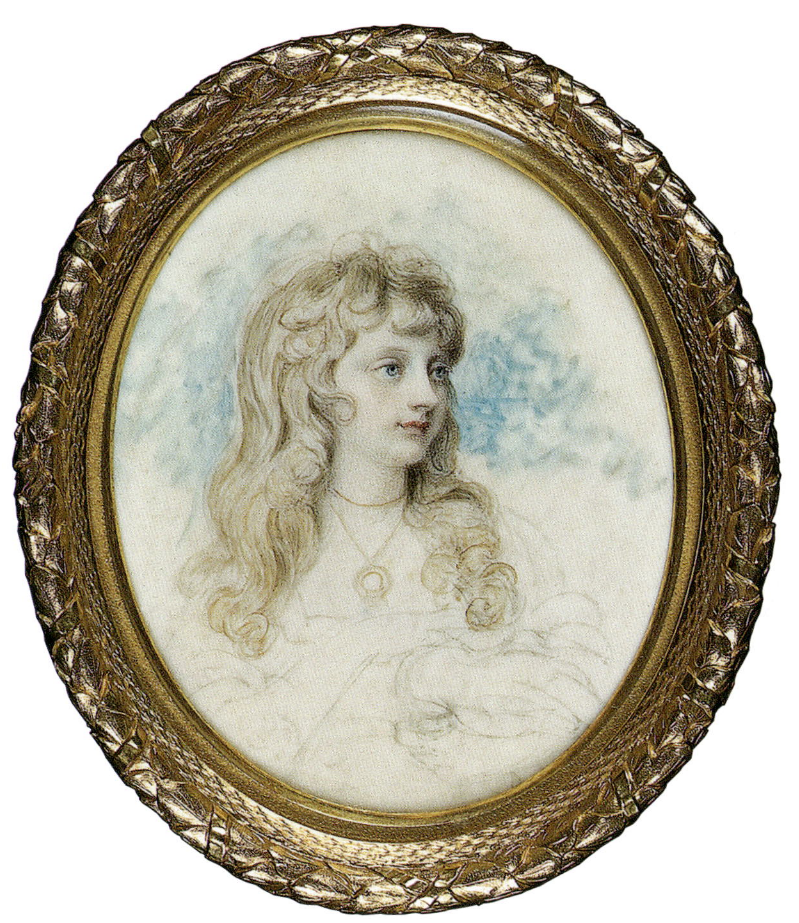

26 *Princess Charlotte of Wales*

1799, 6.6 cm
The Royal Collection © 2004, Her Majesty Queen Elizabeth II
Refs: Edinburgh and London 1995–6, p.125, no.134 and p.86, col. pl.86; Lloyd 2004, pp.198
and 207, fig.110; *Oxford DNB* 2004

Princess Charlotte of Wales (1796–1817) was the only child of the Prince
of Wales, later George IV, and his wife Princess Caroline of Brunswick.
The miniature was painted in 1799 for the sitter's father, who was
charged twenty-five guineas for the work. The original gold filigree
frame, which incorporates a miniature of the Prince of Wales after
Cosway on the back, was commissioned by the Prince that same year
from the leading London goldsmiths Rundell and Bridge, at a further
cost of thirty guineas. Also in 1799, Cosway painted a similarly posed
miniature of Princess Charlotte, which is preserved at Anglesey Abbey,
near Cambridge (National Trust).

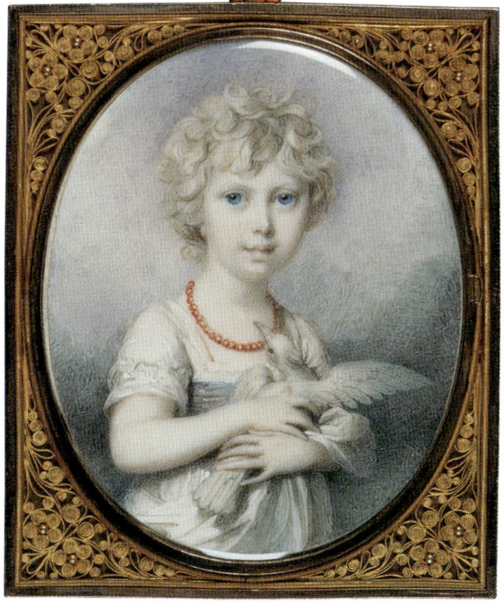

27 *Louis-Philippe, duc d'Orléans* (later King of France)

*c.*1804–5, 5.3 cm
The Royal Collection © 2004, Her Majesty Queen Elizabeth II
Ref: Edinburgh and London 1995–6, p.129, no.178 and p.87, col. pl.92

Louis-Philippe (1773–1850) was the eldest son of Louis-Philippe, duc
d'Orléans (1747–93), known during the Revolution as Philippe-Egalité,
who had been a patron of the artist during his visit to France in 1786. In
1830 Louis-Philippe was proclaimed King of France in succession to the
deposed Charles X. Cosway portrayed the sitter wearing armour and a
purple pelisse fastened to his right shoulder in an octagonal miniature.
This is datable during the Orléans family's exile at Twickenham between
1800 and 1806. A drawing by Henry Bone, dated February 1805, for an
enamel copy of this portrait survives (National Portrait Gallery, London).
A similarly posed and dated oval portrait miniature of this sitter by
Cosway also exists (Cleveland Museum of Art, Ohio), although there he
is not shown wearing armour.

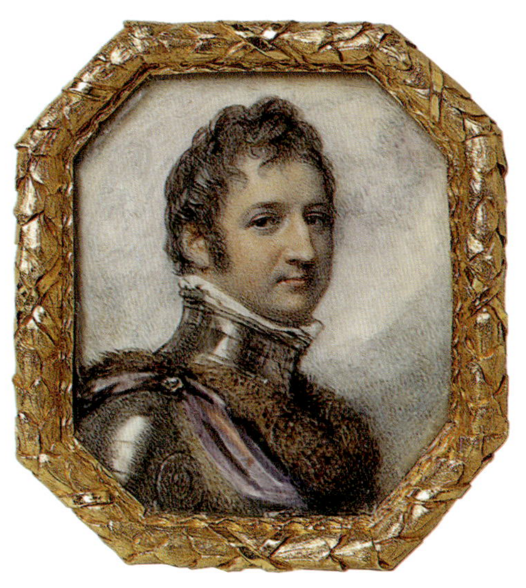

28 *Arthur Wellesley* (later 1st Duke of Wellington)

1808, 7.1 cm
V&A Images,
Victoria and Albert Museum, London
Ref: Edinburgh and London 1995–6, p.129, no.181 and p.87, col. pl.94; *Oxford DNB* 2004

Arthur Wellesley, 1st Duke of Wellington (1769–1852), Field-Marshal, victor at Waterloo, and Prime Minister, was portrayed here in the scarlet and gold-braided coat of the 33rd Regiment. The sitting to Cosway took place just prior to his departure for the Peninsular War campaign. The artist's intimate portrayal of Wellington, which is fully signed and dated on the back, can be compared instructively to three other more famous representations of the sitter: the haunted soldier shown in the portrait oil and drawing by Goya (National Gallery, London, and British Museum, London) and the triumphant half-length oil of 1815–16 by Sir Thomas Lawrence (Apsley House).

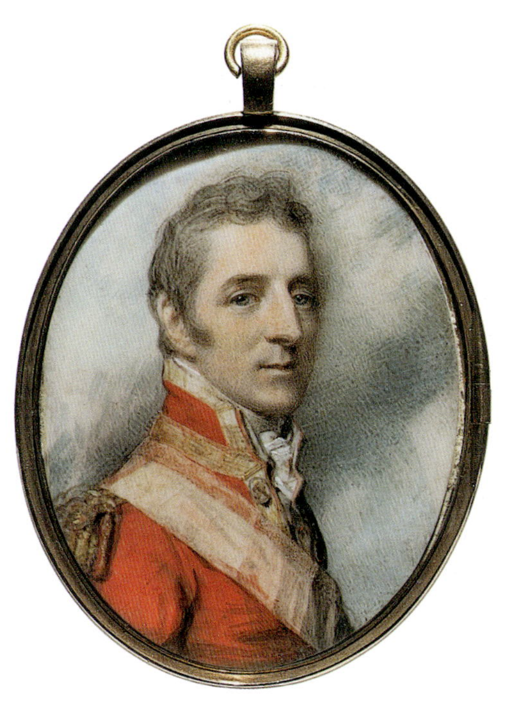

29 *John Philip Kemble*

*c.*1810, 7 cm
V&A Images,
Victoria and Albert Museum, London
Ref: Edinburgh and London 1995–6, p.124, no.126 and p.87, col. pl.93; *Oxford DNB* 2004

John Philip Kemble (1757–1823), brother of the actress Sarah Siddons, was one of the most famous stage actors in Regency Britain, excelling in roles from Shakespearean tragedy. Here, in a late miniature, Cosway depicted Kemble in the *all'antica* dress of one of the actor's most famous roles, Coriolanus. Sir Thomas Lawrence, who had also portrayed Kemble in that role in a full-length oil portrait of 1798 (Guildhall Art Gallery, London), remarked to his fellow-artist Joseph Farington: 'There had been no other countenance as that of Kemble. If 1000 men were collected together you wd be struck with the fire of Kemble' (Farington, *Diary*, 16 July 1810).

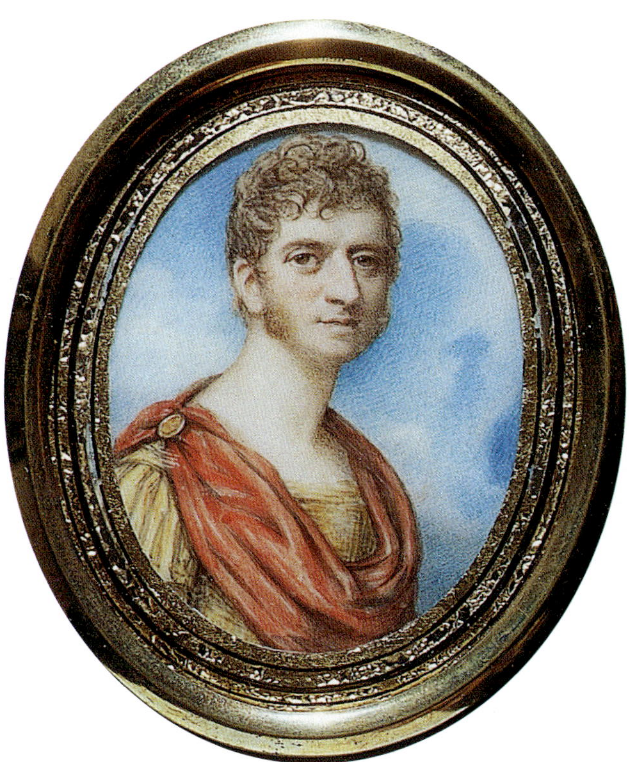

30 *Self-portrait in old age*

*c.*1810, 6 cm
Fitzwilliam Museum, Cambridge
Ref: Edinburgh and London 1995–6, p.129, no.182 and p.87, col. pl.95

This is Cosway's last known self-portrait in miniature. It is marked by an unusual restraint and sombre introspection, contrasting with the flamboyant depictions of his younger self. During the last two decades of his life, Cosway immersed himself increasingly in Christian mysticism and the occult. In two other contemporary late self-portrait drawings he revealed himself alongside Masonic and Judaic symbols. In his first half-length image as a mystic Cosway holds a manuscript volume illustrated with a Star of David (frontispiece; Worcester Art Museum, Massachusetts); while the second drawing is a bizarre full-length portrait in which the artist presented himself as an Old Testament figure, standing over an inscription, which alludes to his name as Esau (Galleria degli Uffizi, Florence). Another autograph version of this self-portrait in miniature was sold at auction recently (Phillips, London, 16 July 1996, lot 178).

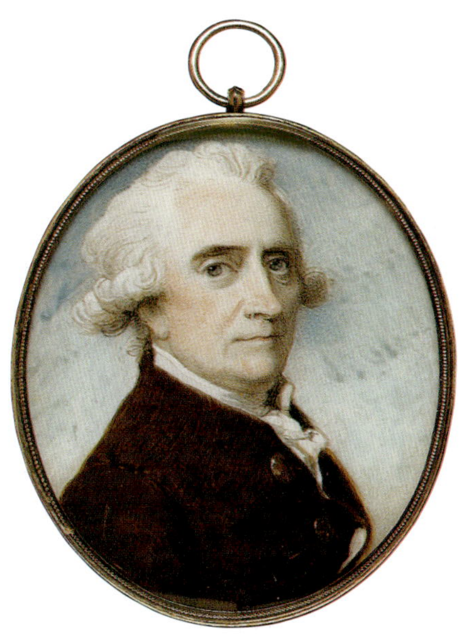

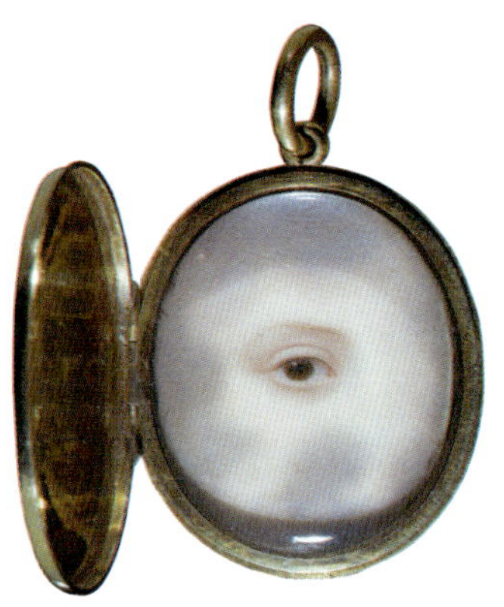

Bibliography

ALLAN 1979
D.G.C.Allan, *William Shipley, Founder of the Royal Society of Arts: A Biography with Documents*, 2nd edn, London, 1979 (1st edn, London, 1968)

ASLESON and BENNETT 2001
Robyn Asleson and Shelley M. Bennett, *British Paintings at The Huntington*, San Marino, New Haven and London, 2001

BARNETT 1995
Gerald Barnett, *Richard and Maria Cosway: A Biography*, Tiverton, 1995

BAYNE-POWELL 1985
Robert Bayne-Powell, *Catalogue of Portrait Miniatures in the Fitzwilliam Museum, Cambridge*, Cambridge, 1985

BRYANT 2003
Julius Bryant, *Kenwood*: *Paintings in the Iveagh Bequest*, New Haven and London, 2003

COOMBS 1998
Katherine Coombs, *The Portrait Miniature in England*, London, 1998
(2nd edn, London, 2005)

COSWAY 1791
[Richard Cosway], *A Catalogue of the Entire Collection of Pictures of Richard Cosway, Esq. R.A. Principal Painter to His Royal Highness The Prince of Wales, in the Great Saloon, and eight other Apartments, of his House in Pall Mall, containing the Undoubted Works of the Great Masters of the Florentine, Venetian, Lombard, Flemish, and Dutch Schools*, London, 1791

CUNNINGHAM 1829–33
Allan Cunningham, *The Lives of the Most Eminent British Painters, Sculptors, and Architects*, London, 1829–33

DANIELL 1890
Frederick B. Daniell, *A Catalogue Raisonné of the Engraved Works of Richard Cosway, R.A.*, London, 1890

EDINBURGH and LONDON 1995–6
Richard and Maria Cosway: Regency Artists of Taste and Fashion, exhibition catalogue,
ed. Stephen Lloyd, Scottish National Portrait Gallery, Edinburgh, 1995 (exhibition travelled
to National Portrait Gallery, London, 1995–6)

EDINBURGH 1996–7
Portrait Miniatures from the Collection of The Duke of Buccleuch, exhibition catalogue, by
Stephen Lloyd, Scottish National Portrait Gallery, Edinburgh, 1996–7

EDINBURGH 1999
Raeburn's Rival: Archibald Skirving (1749–1819), exhibition catalogue, by Stephen Lloyd,
Scottish National Portrait Gallery, Edinburgh, 1999

FARINGTON 1978–84
Joseph Farington: The Diary of Joseph Farington, eds. Kenneth Garlick, Angus Macintrye and
Kathryn Cave, 16 vols, New Haven and London, 1978–84 (Index compiled by Evelyn
Newby, New Haven and London, 1998)

FOREMAN 1998
Amanda Foreman, *Georgiana, Duchess of Devonshire*, London, 1998

FOSKETT 1987
Daphne Foskett, *Miniatures: Dictionary and Guide*, Woodbridge, 1987

FRASER 2004
Flora Fraser, *Princesses: The six daughters of George III*, London, 2004

HAZLITT 1822
William Hazlitt, 'Fonthill Abbey', *The London Magazine*, November 1822, pp.173–80

HAZLITT 1826
William Hazlitt, 'On the Old Age of Artists', *The Plain Speaker: opinions on books, men and
things*, 2 vols, London, 1826, I, pp.207–27

HAZLITT 1930–4
William Hazlitt, *The Complete Works of…*, ed. P.P.Howe, 21 vols., London, 1930–4

HICKEY 1923–5
William Hickey, *Memoirs of…*, ed. Alfred Spencer, 4 vols., London, 1923–5

LIBRARY OF THE FINE ARTS 1832
[Anon.], 'Recollections of Richard Cosway, Esq. R.A.', *Library of the Fine Arts*, 4 vols., London, 1832, IV, pp.184–91

LLOYD 1991
Stephen Lloyd, 'Richard Cosway, RA: the artist as collector, connoisseur and *virtuoso*', *Apollo*, CXXXIII, no.352, June 1991, pp.398–405

LLOYD 1995
Stephen Lloyd, 'Fashioning the image of the Prince: Richard Cosway and George IV', *'Squanderous and Lavish Profusion': George IV, his image and patronage of the arts*, ed. Dana Arnold, London, 1995, pp.5–14

LLOYD 1998
Stephen Lloyd, 'Richard Cosway: "Primarius Pictor", collezionista e virtuoso', *Maria e Richard Cosway*, ed. Tino Gipponi, Turin, 1998, pp.45–68

LLOYD 2004
Stephen Lloyd, 'The Cosway Inventory of 1820: listing unpaid commissions and the contents of 20 Stratford Place, Oxford Street, London', *Walpole Society*, LXVI, 2004, pp.163–217

LONDON 1895
Catalogue of Miniatures, Oil Paintings, Drawings and Engravings by Richard Cosway, R.A. (1740–1821) and Maria Cosway his Wife, exhibition catalogue, ed. George C. Williamson, Moncorvo House [South Kensington], London, 1895

MELBOURNE 1983
The Great Eighteenth Century Exhibition, exhibition catalogue, by Jane Clark, National Gallery of Victoria, Melbourne, 1983

MILLAR 1996
Oliver Millar, 'George IV when Prince of Wales: his debts to artists and craftsmen'

(Documents for the History of Collecting: 2), *The Burlington Magazine*, CXXXVIII , no.1001, August 1986, pp.586–92

NEW YORK 1996
European Miniatures in The Metropolitan Museum of Art, exhibition catalogue, by Graham Reynolds and Katharine Baetjer, Metropolitan Museum of Art, New York, 1996

NEW YORK *et al* 1996–7
Masterpieces in Little: Portrait Miniatures from the Collection of Her Majesty Queen Elizabeth II, exhibition catalogue, by Christopher Lloyd and Vanessa Remington, Metropolitan Museum of Art, New York (and three other venues), 1996–7

NOON *et al* 1981
John Murdoch, Jim Murrell, Patrick J. Noon and Roy Strong, *The English Miniature*, New Haven and London, 1981, pp.163–209

OXFORD DNB 2004
H.C.G. Matthew and Brian Harrison (eds), *Oxford Dictionary of National Biography*, 60 vols, Oxford, 2004

PARISSIEN 2001
Steven Parissien, *George IV: The Grand Entertainment*, London, 2001

REYNOLDS 1980
Graham Reynolds, *Wallace Collection: Catalogue of Portrait Miniatures*, London, 1980

REYNOLDS 1988
Graham Reynolds, *English Portrait Miniatures*, 2nd edn, Cambridge, 1988
(1st edn, London, 1952)

REYNOLDS 1992
Graham Reynolds, 'Late Eighteenth-Century Miniatures by Richard Cosway and Andrew Plimer', *British Art 1740–1820: Essays in Honor of Robert R. Wark*, ed. Guilland Sutherland, San Marino, California, 1992

SMITH 1828
J.T. Smith, *Nollekens and his Times: comprehending a life of that celebrated sculptor; and memoirs of several contemporary artists…*, 2 vols, London, 1828

WALKER 1992
Richard Walker, *The Eighteenth and Early Nineteenth Century Miniatures in the Collection of Her Majesty The Queen*, Cambridge, 1992

WALKER 1998
Richard Walker, *Miniatures: 300 years of the English Miniature illustrated from the collections of the National Portrait Gallery*, London, 1998

WILLIAMSON 1897
George C. Williamson, *Richard Cosway, R.A. and his Wife and Pupils: Miniaturists of the Eighteenth Century*, London, 1897

WILLIAMSON 1905
George C. Williamson, *Richard Cosway, R.A.*, London, 1905

WILLIAMSON 1906–8
George C. Williamson, *Catalogue of the Collection of the Miniatures, the Property of J. Pierpont Morgan*, 4 vols, London, 1906–8

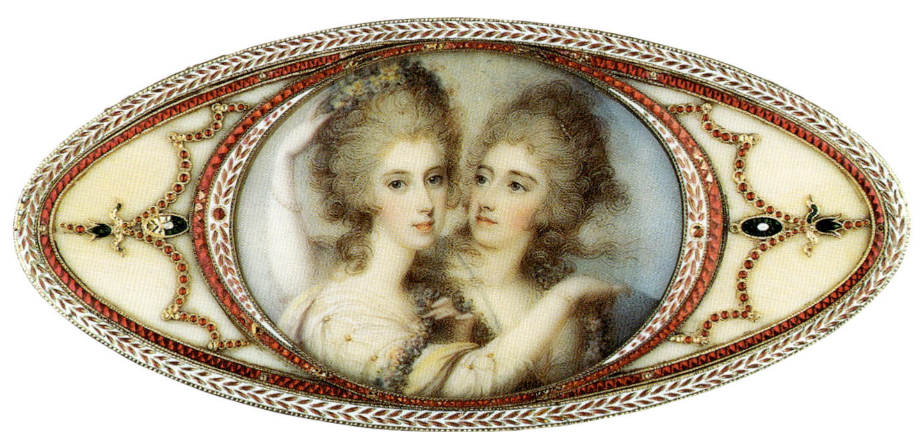

Index

The roman numbers refer to text. References to miniatures are in bold.